How to Attract *Significantly* More Customers

... in good times and bad!

This book contains Seven Secrets business leaders need to know in order to attract *significantly* more "A" customers.

Abstract: If you run a company and are not sure if your marketing and sales efforts are bringing in as many customers as you think they should, this book is for you. Perhaps you are not sure how much *should* be spent on trade shows, advertisements, PR, etc.

Or, if you are looking to turbo-charge your sales and have tried different kinds of sales training, have brought in several consultants and/or marketing firms to boost revenue – without the results you would like to see, then this book is for you.

How to Attract *Significantly* More Customers is copyright © 2008, Mark Paul. All rights reserved. Printed in the United States of America. No part of this book may be used or reproduced in any manner, in physical or electronic format without the prior written permission of the publisher and author, except in the case of reprints in the context of reviews (maximum 250 words). Please be aware that the techniques described in this book must be appropriately tailored by users to fit specific needs. This book does *not* provide any legal nor accounting advice. Please seek the counsel of attorneys for legal advice. For information, write to Cedar Mill Publishing, Post Office Box 91507, Portland, Oregon, 97291-0507, U.S.A.

Paul, Mark
    How to Attract Significantly More Customers
    First edition, first printing
    EAN: 978-0-9708665-7-8 / ISBN: 0-9708665-7-7

Publisher's note: The process outlined in this book works so well it is **patent-pending!** *Purchasers can use the concepts and processes internal to their own company, but may not license, sell or give them to any third party without prior approval.*

How to Attract Significantly More Customers... in good times & bad

Forward

A picture may be worth a thousand words, but implementing the concepts in this book could be worth millions to your business. Whether you're implementing a new strategy or re-tuning an old one, you want measurable results.

Mark personally worked with us to implement these concepts in our company, significantly increasing revenue, upping the valuation by millions, and ultimately helping us achieve our business objectives.

Don't just read this book. Implement the concepts, measure the results, and enjoy the ride!

Don Dunstan   CEO of US Software,
acquired by Lantronix

Introduction

Stop the Madness!

What goes on in some companies can best be described as madness. On two fronts: First, many companies tend to spend a lot on marketing – trying new things all the time – without knowing what the outcomes have been or will be. Nor the probable return on investment (ROI). If the company is doing four marketing things (that aren't working to the company's satisfaction), what do they do? They try a fifth thing (read: marketing tactic). This only cuts your "marketing dollar" from 25 cents per tactic to 20 cents per tactic. If one tactic provides a much higher ROI than another, why do any other tactics – than that one?

Second, many companies rely on gut feel instead of asking the difficult question "How can we spend *even less*, while generating more qualified leads, with shorter sales cycles?" And instead of collecting and then managing by facts.

This book is about considering the *entire* customer-attraction process in a completely different way. A way that will enable you to get better results while (typically) spending *less*.

Attract Better Customers = Increase Corporate Valuation

The concepts in this book – when implemented to their fullest – have resulted in companies dramatically boosting their revenue, profitability and cash position. They have also helped several company owners become millionaires, due to increases in corporate valuatin resulting from applying *all* seven secrets and the subsequent acquisition of their companies.

This book will help your company:
- Attract more Customers, Clients, and Members
- Reduce your sales cycles
- Find more "A" customers who pay sooner

- Typically *reduce* your marketing & sales costs
- Define better products and services
- In good times & bad!

What Works, What Doesn't

This book works whether your Customers are consumers or businesses. In fact, non-profits / associations can use the principles in this book to attract more members! A graduate institute even applied several of these secrets to quadruple their student base.

This book will help you focus your outbound marketing & sales tactics by *finding out* which few tactics provide the highest return on your investment. In your industry, with your products / services, and in your market niche. The concepts in this book usually result in *fewer* marketing tactics being employed – which can save you time and money.

> Real-world examples are provided – to help you envision how to implement each Secret. They are identified within each chapter by a box.

Not a Sales-Training, nor a How-To Marketing book

This book has nothing to do with sales training, "cultural" aspects of a sales organization, nor is it a "tactical" how-to book of marketing methods proliferating the marketplace.

As you read this, please be aware that the first few secrets can be perceived as "ethereal", while the last few can be considered "too analytic". Therein lies the power of integrating *all* secrets. And how they all work *together*. So, if you feel the first few secrets seem mushy, they will all synergize later.

How to Read This Book

You may want to read through the entire book once – just to get its feel & concepts. Then read it again, more slowly to better understand how all secrets work together. Unlike my prior book,

"The Entrepreneur's Survival Guide" – where each chapter is a stand-alone reference – all seven secrets need to work *together*, or the results will not be nearly as great. Please be sure to take time to answer the questions that will be asked in this book.

Why "Good times, and bad"?

The concepts and processes described in this book have been successfully applied to companies at various stages of their growth cycle and different stages of the economic cycle. These concepts and processes allow companies to better understand how customers think, *especially* when times change.

Concepts May Even Help You Reduce Costs

Every company I've helped has limited resources. This book is not intended to help you "go green", however you can determine ways to reduce your spending which typically result in less waste – a green concept – to help you improve your triple-bottom-line.

For Company Leaders

This book is primarily for CEOs / business owners / General Managers. It is about how they can turbo-charge their marketing and sales efforts to attract significantly more customers. However, marketing and sales executives can also benefit from this book.

The tenets in the book have everything to do with helping the person-in-charge *create an environment* for marketing and sales executives & teams to outperform themselves by turbo-charging their customer-attraction process. Once you embrace the concept and process, whoever is responsible for marketing can then be even more successful.

I hope to help small & large companies alike kick-start their progression to their next levels – in a way that is a "win" for the company, its employees, executives, and customers.

Mark Paul - Portland, Oregon – March, 2008

How to Attract *Significantly* More Customers
... in good times & bad!

Preface: *Why Seven Secrets?*
1. (To be revealed later)
2. Be 100% Open to Change & Learning
3. Assume Nothing
4. Recognize You May Need to Learn a New Language
5. Assess Your Company's Current Performance
6. Ask Your Customers / Prospects What *You* Need to Know
7. Test Your Assumptions
8. Bonus Secret

Addenda:
- #1: Real-world Examples
- #2: Seven Secrets Summarized
- #3: How to Get Your Data Analyzed
- #4: Products & Services to Help Your Company Grow

How to Attract Significantly More Customers… in good times & bad

Preface:
Why Seven Secrets?

Isn't attracting customers all about feet on the street, cold calling, making sales presentations, "who you know, not what you know", and offering better products at a lower cost? Won't doing these things help your product or service sell itself?

Well, yes and no.

There are hundreds of books on how to sell better. There are also books on how to make advertising and direct mail more effective. Additionlly, there are millions of sales and marketing people - most are seemingly consultants.

So how do you determine *which* book to buy, read and implement, or *which* consultant to listen to? Or decide *which* sales & marketing approach to implement?

It isn't easy. If it were, you wouldn't have bought (or browsed through) this book.

Overrun with ideas

Most books and consultants who deal with marketing and sales are focused on improving their sales or marketing team performance. They conduct sales training, help companies with trade shows, advertising, public relations (PR), or help improve cold calling, plus a variety of other tactically focused efforts. Many of these books and consultants indeed provide tremendous insights into how to improve sales and/or marketing teams' performance.

This book is *not at all* about training sales people in the latest closing techniques. It is *not* about helping you with your branding. It doesn't discuss what color your logo should be, or how to improve direct mail response rates.

This book *can* help you uncover *which* marketing and sales techniques work for you and which are a waste of your time and money so you can focus only on those tactics that work for

- *your* company ,
- *your* products and services,
- *your* industry,
- *your* market niche, and
- *your* customers.

If you are not your company's CEO: Read it, then give this book to him/her. It will make *your* life easier!

This book was primarily written to help CEOs* determine what they *must do*, in order to attract significantly more customers. It will help the person-in-charge answer the questions that keep him/her up at night: "Why aren't we selling more?" "Are our marketing dollars being spent effectively?" "How can I *know* that a new marketing initiative will actually bring in more customers?" "Will doing this new sales push really bring in the *best* customers?"

* For ease of writing and reading, I will refer to the person in charge: CEO / President, business owner, general manager – whoever is responsible for the profit and loss of a company or business unit – as the CEO.

Because of this focus on the CEO, this book tackles the issues of effectiveness not efficiency, and strategy not tactics.

The notion of *"while"*

Specifically, this book outlines the seven things a CEO needs to embrace – in order to enable him/her to attract significantly more customers, *while* (typically) spending less on both marketing and sales! In good times and bad.

The real questions CEOs need to answer have nothing to do with spending *more* on marketing and sales. Anyone can do that! Instead, their goal is to make significant improvements in return-on-investment (ROI), *while* spending less on marketing and sales. And in a way that helps your marketing and sales people actually welcome these improvements.

This requires a strategic approach. And it requires that the CEO embrace seven secrets, learn them, implement them, and insist that everyone in their marketing and sales departments learn and implement them.

Your life will be easier and your company will turbo-charge your customer-attraction process.

So, why are there *seven* secrets?

As a consultant and interim executive for the past 19 years, I have first-hand experience in developing and then applying these secrets. (Appendix 1 has examples of the results achieved using these secrets.) Without integrating *all* of the secrets, the general effectiveness is far lower than when the seven are embraced – together.

Also - since dramatically improving your customer-attraction ability requires buy-in by the CEO (quite often the founder of the company), there are three and half "personal" secrets and three and a half "business" secrets.

In order to work, the *personal* secrets demand that CEOs take an objective look at themselves. This can be extremely difficult, yet is essential for CEOs to get on a path of personal enlightenment so they can more effectively lead a new way of attracting *significantly* more "A" customers.

These personal secrets may seem like you've heard them all before, and it will be easy to jump to conclusions about what they mean. Rest assured, until you read the entire book – and see how these secrets work together to provide you the results you want – each secret independently will not be as powerful as when you embrace and implement them all.

The *business* secrets work together to help your organization attract more customers, better customers, and sooner. The business secrets provide a business process that can be put into gear relatively easily and replicated as the market shifts.

There are seven because that's just how it worked out, though I do consider them somewhat lucky.

Secret #1
To be revealed, shortly

Before turning the page and reading any more of this book, you will need to do something that is *extremely* important. If you fail to do this, the lesson in this chapter will not be as powerful as it could be. In fact, this one lesson may be worth hundreds of times the price of this book!

Please take out a piece of paper and answer the question below. List as many items as you can think of in two or three minutes.

Question: *"What strategic marketing things have you done, or are you doing now, to attract more customers?"*

Please do not turn the page until you have finished writing your list.

If you have turned the page and have not yet developed your list, please do so now.

This first step is absolutely essential for you to learn the first secret. Without listing your current strategic efforts, you are robbing yourself of a lesson that could last you the rest of your life!

So – please answer the question: *"What strategic marketing things have you done, or are you doing now, to attract more customers?"* List as many as you can think of.

(The reason I am being bold and assuming you are continuing to read on, is because I do it all the time!)

Do not turn the page until you are done with your assignment.

If you have your list put together, please read on. Your list may have some or most of the following:

- Advertising
- Brochures
- Billboards
- Catalogs
- Direct mail
- Distributors
- Email marketing
- Networking
- Newsletters
- Phonebook / Yellowpages
- Presentations
- Prior experience
- Public relations
- Public speaking
- Referral / word of mouth
- Requests for proposal
- Seminars
- Send sample(s)
- Sky writing
- Trade associations
- Trade shows
- Website

Typically, companies I work with implement five or more of these efforts in their marketing. Does your list look something like this? Is it a listing of marketing *tactics*? I did not ask you to list tactics. I asked you to list "strategic marketing things". I asked it that way for a reason.

> You are in good company. Having presented in front of hundreds of CEOs over the years, in nearly *every* case, the answers they provided included a list of tactics. Those listed above, and more. (I added skywriting! ☺)

You are now ready for Secret #1, which is the half personal and half business-oriented secret:

Secret #1: Recognize the difference between *strategic* marketing and *tactical* marketing.

We will get into this difference – in spades – later in this book. For now, the important thing is that you *recognize* that you may well be thinking tactically, when the real value you can add to your company is to think strategically.

Tactical marketing is akin to "doing stuff", while strategic marketing will get you results. Big difference. The first (tactical) provides a great way to spend money. It might be productive or not, but it *will* use your limited resources. Quickly. Taking a strategic approach will enable you to learn which marketing tactics (among other things) will yield the highest return on investment. Being effective (doing the right thing), vs. being efficient (doing things right).

Simply *recognizing* the difference between strategy and tactics, you will be far along in your journey to attract significantly more "A" customers. In good times, and bad.

Three real-life examples where taking a strategic approach (vs. a tactical approach) yielded the following results:

	Company A	Company B	Company C
Before	$100K/month	$1 million	7.5 months
After	$171K/month	$17 million	2 months
	Gross revenue	Valuation	Sales cycle
Time to achieve these results?	3 months	6 months	4 months

Note: The "personal" side of the secret has to do with the implied "You" in the secret: ***You have to*** *recognize the difference* between strategic marketing and tactical marketing. The "business" side of this secret has to do with recognizing the ***difference*** between strategic and tactical marketing.

Secret #2
Be 100% Open to Change & Learning

How hard could this be? Really? The answer is: Extremely!

The reason "100%" is used, is to help you get off "top-dead center". We are all a little open to change and learning. Especially those who have lived the life of an entrepreneur or executive. Someone who has been a founder of a company probably thrives on change. But most likely, as the CEO, you like to create change and disruption – for others.

If you have a new product or service; something unique that adds significant value to others, whether they are companies or people, you may expect them to change *their* behavior in order to adopt your product or service. As you know, this isn't easy. In fact, getting people to "get" the value of your solution is a difficult challenge. Why? Because people do not like changing! Being human, it may not be easy to adapt to others' ways of thinking, nor for *you* to change. It sure isn't for me.

Saturday Night Live had a skit with a couple cavemen. They were crouched behind a rock, and lightning had just struck some brush, causing a fire. One turned to the other and said:

> *"It's new. Therefore I fear it. Therefore it's bad."*

This sums up our fear of change succinctly. We like what we know, what's familiar. What makes us comfortable, even if it doesn't really work for us. The "new" can cause anxiety, and we tend to avoid anxiety whenever possible. When I present to a group of CEOs, I ask "Who here is open to change?" Almost everyone raises their hands. However, human (i.e., animal) instinct is to quickly recognize differences around us to protect ourselves.

An example that proves we all live in the "dream of the planet*" where change is difficult – can be summed up thusly: People used to think the Earth was flat. Anyone saying otherwise was shunned or stoned. We all believed "group-think" and (obviously) must have feared the change that would occur if we *learned* that we are not the center of the universe. This went on for millennia! Talk about not wanting to accept change.

Another example? Just think of political candidates and their completely different views on how to solve difficult problems. No one seems to really listen, because to act on what they hear would require change. Perhaps their (and our) resistance to change is because "Change dishonors our past".

On a much smaller scale, this is true for all people. There is nothing wrong with not being open to hearing another side. Unless doing so puts your company at risk, or causes your company to avoid potential sources of new, unique and valuable ideas – that could turbo-charge it to its next several levels.

We might say we want something, but do we really?

> After several weeks of helping a client, she asked me to review some reports and make improvements. Then she said something that floored me: *"Just don't make any changes.*

---

* To read more about the notion of the "dream of the planet", please refer to *The Four Agreements*, by Don Miguel Ruiz. ISBN 1-878424-31-9

> By definition, improvement = change. How can one improve *any*thing, without changing it? Whether it's just a little or 180^0 in a different direction? I immediately handed back the report to her and then had a discussion: If she *really* wanted to improve it or just wanted some sort of stamp of approval. When she realized that her fear of change manifested itself in the "no change" statement, she recanted, laughed and was able to move forward. What was important was *improvement*. Change is just a vehicle for improvement.

Recall that old saying – without being open to change, "doing what you've always done will get you what you've always got!" CEOs have the biggest *potential* for resistance to change. Why? Because quite often, the whole reason the company or organization exists and becomes successful is due to the founder / CEO. S/He has created the organization, led it to where it is now, and has learned a lot along the way. They've had to make tough choices, usually with insufficient information and (if the company is still growing), those decisions have been generally correct.

However, the more one is right, the more one can start making assumptions (next chapter), and being less open to something new (i.e., change). To illustrate this point, the following analogy is excerpted from The Entrepreneur's Survival Guide*:

> "Initially, if you plot the entrepreneur's or CEO's abilities over that of a fast-growth company's performance, the leader *is the reason* the company thrives. The drive and stewardship exhibited by the founder lifts the company's performance and causes growth. That is, the leader *pulls up* company performance. But as the company adds more people, competition becomes more complex, and the market more sophisticated, the company gradually becomes more difficult to manage. If the leader's capabilities do not outpace that

of the company's, then the leader *pulls down* company performance."

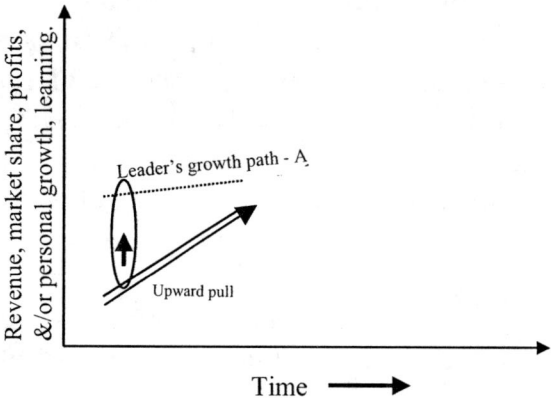

Initially, the leader pulls company performance up.

"Leaders have limitations. The more defensive you are in challenging your own limitations, the more difficult it is for you to learn, adapt, and continue to be of immense value to your company."

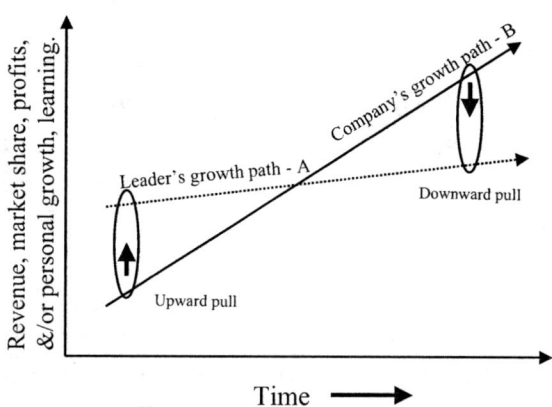

Often, the leader can also pull performance down.

Careful what you *say* you want

Although I try to *not* hire a client until/unless I know they're open to change, I'm not always successful. Many clients *said* they wanted to accomplish aggressive goals, but the changes required were too great. They went right back to their old habits/what they knew, and felt comfortable with. It's human nature. So you see that change is, in fact, extremely difficult. Therefore, it is one of the seven secrets, because just knowing that you might be resistant to something new may be enough to give you pause – to wait before rejecting something out of hand.

The difference between a Gold Medallist and Silver Medallist (for instance in a 100-meter dash) is often just fractions of a second. If a simple adjustment to a person's gate, stride, breathing or focus can make the difference between gold and silver, perhaps a slight adjustment in your customer attraction process can mean all the difference between struggling to make payroll and building a thriving company, sought after by your best customers – and potential acquirers.

Please think about your answers to the "strategic marketing" question. If you currently present at trade shows, and you discover that direct marketing would yield 100% improvement, would you change? Or – if you spend a bulk of your marketing budget on advertising, but a referral approach would yield significantly more customers, would you change?

My point? Recognize that getting different results usually means doing something different. Make sure that you want what you say you want! Then remove "fear-of-change" roadblocks, including your own!

Secret #3
Assume Nothing

This is a corollary to the last secret, and is integrative with the rest. This secret is so important, that if you do not heed it, the results you obtain from Secrets # 5 & #6 (later in the book) will be of little value to you. That would be a terrible mistake: If you are *serious* about attracting significantly more "A" customers.

As Will Rogers said: "It's not what we *don't know* that hurts us, it's *what we know that ain't so.*"

CEOs tend to be very smart people. So smart, that quite often they have had to fill in the gaps in order to make timely decisions. Successful CEOs develop a knack for making pretty good decisions based on insufficient information. They do it out of habit and necessity.

We rarely have enough information to make perfect decisions, and therefore have to make assumptions. It happens so many times during a day that we don't even realize we're doing it. Besides, who has time to get all the information before making a decision? Doing research, assessing it, gathering others' opinions, and learning what they've learned slows down an organization and may even cripple it. Or so it seems.

Which is exactly why – *in the case of doing what is needed to attract* significantly *more "A" customers* in good times and bad – CEOs need to check their assumptions at the door. Forgetting to do this important step will blind you to the information you will obtain in Secrets 5, 6, and 7.

My point? Things change! What worked before may not work again. What you assumed before may not be valid now. Assumptions can be habitual -- and can be fatal to your company!

> One of my clients was in the embedded software industry. There were (and still are) two major trade shows worldwide, with eight other important shows and many more smaller ones. The "dream of the industry" was (and still is), *"If you do not show up at trade shows, everyone will think you're out of business, or going out of business and they will stop buying from you."*
>
> My client spent 75% of his marketing budget on trade shows every year as a result. By using the other secrets in this book, we found out that [1] every $1 spent gained 50 cents in gross revenue (thank goodness for that other 25% of the marketing budget!), [2] the close ratio for telesales follow-up on the thousands of trade-show leads being generated was 1.47% (I'll always remember that number), [3] on a list of 18 ways that my client's customers bought (how they made buying decisions), trade shows was #18 (last!) and "calls from telesales people" was #17.
>
> My client was using the two worst ways possible to sell. No wonder he needed help. It wasn't his fault. It was the "dream of the industry". Everyone in the industry made a big deal out of these trade shows, spending tens of millions of dollars every year – gaining lots of "leads".

More on this example will be provided later in this book.

Are you making any assumptions about your customers?

Secret #4
Recognize You May Need to Learn a New Language

> I once had a client in the health services business, who signed with me not because I had any experience in his industry, but because of some functional expertise (product development / program management).
>
> As we got further along the engagement, I realized I didn't really understand when he started talking about "protocol this", and "protocol that". It didn't take too long to figure it out (I asked him) that in healthcare, *protocol* ("A set of guidelines or rules") is close to another term, *process* ("A designed sequence of attributes of a system").
>
> Quite often, he would use protocol for process. This represents a different language. Imagine if that one word were required in order for me to land this client. It would not have happened.

Secrets # 5, 6 and 7 may require that you learn a new language. Why? Because your customers don't care about *your* language! They don't even care about your products and services. They only care about what your products and service *can do for them*. It is way beyond the difference between selling features and selling benefits.

A graphic may explain what I mean:

Feature	Benefit	Motivation / Value
Cell phone	I can call from the road	In case I get stranded
Cell phone with camera	So I can take pictures	If I get in an accident, I'll have a record of what happened, for insurance
Cell phone from Verizon	Because of free "in"-calling	So I can talk with family without having to pay extra

In the cases above, it is the underlying motivation, or value people receive that drives the language they use. Or it could be pain/risk avoidance.

Being able to sync up with prospective customers is all about getting to the very core of their *motivation* for buying products and services – *from you* – in the first place. Know this and you will know what you need in order to attract significantly more "A" customers. Fail to learn *their language*, and it will remain very costly for you to persuade people to buy.

As your significant other might say – in the role of a potential customer – "It's not about you, it's about me."

This is a very subtle secret.

Customers only care that what they buy (perhaps what you sell) will help them -- in some way. You are no different. You want the water you drink to be pure, easily accessible (always "on"), and low priced. If you want a truck, it may be to haul things: Certain things, in a certain way, that meet *your* needs, and solve *your* problems. You (may) want golf clubs to help you drive straight… which is more important than what they're made out of. If cardboard helped me shoot straighter, farther, with more accuracy, I'd buy that over carbon fiber. I don't care about technology, I care about what technology *will do for me*.

> When I first started consulting, I was selling Project Management training and consulting. No one seemed to buy. It wasn't until I stopped assuming everyone knew what I knew (that project management organizations and processes can make a significant difference in getting products to market in record time); it wasn't until I was open to changing my attitude and perspective on what I was doing, that I was able to *listen* to my prospective clients. And what did they tell me? They wanted to develop more, better products and services, *while* spending less time and money, and have their solutions sell like hotcakes. It was all about product development, *not* project management!

I had to learn a new language.

> My client in the embedded software industry (mentioned earlier) had RTOS (Real-time Operating System) software that was very well received, but they were having trouble selling their products in the United States. They had a great reputation, excellent engineering staff and were around a long time (some would say they *started* the commercial embedded software industry, in the 1970s).
>
> When I asked their engineers, marketing and sales people what their major selling point was, they all indicated that their products had very *compact* software. When I asked

> their customers what they valued, it was because of my client's *integrated* software.
>
> Their motivation was simple: Compact – to buy smaller chips – to save money: Worth $1 million. Or Integrated – to reduce the need to hire systems engineers, nor buy from five different vendors, so customers could speed products to market: Worth $10 million.
>
> This one word helped propel the company to a nearly 20x valuation, in about six months!

One word difference = A different language.

My point? You don't have to learn a new language, you simply have to be *open* to learning a new language. If you aren't, you will not be ready for what you will learn by implementing all secrets from this book.

Perhaps you can see how these secrets are starting to work together.

Secret #5
Assess Your Company's Current Performance

If you are ready to recognize the difference between strategic and tactical marketing, open to change and learning, ready to check your assumptions at the door, and able to recognize you may have to learn a new language, then you are ready for this secret. Otherwise, please go back and re-read / re-think the first several chapters. Or sleep on it and come back to this chapter, tomorrow.

Why assess performance?

You may be asking yourself: Why assess what's already been done? How are we going to learn from "water under the bridge"? Because you'll be able to:

- Understand every transition in your sales funnel (and be positioned to optimize them to shorten your sales cycle),
- Understand who your "A" customers are and what your "A" products are (so you know where to focus),
- Understand why lost customers do not buy, and
- Lay the groundwork for understanding the ROI of each of your marketing tactics.

In order to learn what changes are needed (you know - how you're going to improve), you will need to know where you are, how you got here, and learn from *what* you've done – and what you have yet to do to make significant differences in your company's results. (Past behavior = past results. New behavior = new results.)

This step is an assessment of your company's customer-attraction performance. It is not to find blame or string up someone for prior performance. It is to get *you* into a position to attract significantly more customers.

By assessing information you already have, you will not only set yourself up for growth, you will be able to have a baseline "metric", upon which you can then check future performance. If what you do going forward is worse than what you've done, you'll know to stop. If it's better (and it will likely be so), you'll be able to assess *how much* better. You will also be able to measure your marketing and sales performance.

What do we need to measure? And why?

The answer is: It depends. The notion here is *not* to get into analysis-paralysis. It is to gain *enough* insights, so that your decision-making (on how to spend your limited marketing and sales dollars) improves, dramatically. So that your return on investment improves. And, so that your customer-attraction process gets turbo-charged by being built on a solid foundation.

This is not a "financial assessment", although financial records will be reviewed. Personnel performance will *not* be reviewed. This part of the process can be thought of as a marketing and sales assessment, which can help you determine what your team needs to do – from here on.

If you maintain financials in an accounting (software) program, and customer information in a Customer Relationship Management (software) program, you will be well served. If you have neither, this is a big mistake! Some programs to consider are:

- Business One (SAP)
- Clientele (Epicor)
- Mas 90 (Sage)
- Peachtree (Sage)
- Quickbooks (Intuit)
- Quicken (Intuit)

} Accounting Software = Where you've been

- Act! (Sage)
- Compiere (Compiere)
- Goldmine (Frontrange Solutions)
- SalesForce.com (SalesForce.com)
- SugarCRM (SugarCRM)

} Customer Relationship Management Software = Where you're going

If you have none of these software packages but still keep records of financial transactions and notes about your customers & prospective customers, you will be able to proceed with vigor. If you do not, it will be tougher, but still doable.

Questions to consider when preparing for your internal assessment include:

- What does your sales funnel look like?
- Do you even *have* a sales funnel?
    - Is it documented and reviewed periodically?
- Do you have a marketing process?
    - What does it look like? Is it written down?
- Do you have a sales process?
    - What does it look like? Is it written down?
- How much are you spending on marketing? And sales?
    - Is it enough? Too much? How do you know?
- What's your suspect to prospect conversion ratio?

- What is your prospect to close ratio?
- What is your cost to acquire a customer?
- Cost to maintain a customer? Value of a Customer?
    - How do you know?
- What is your Return on Investment (ROI) for each marketing tactic?
- What is your organizational responsibility for marketing?
- How much are you spending, and is it getting results… or are you just "doing stuff?"
- What are your objectives for *each* marketing tactic?

This may seem daunting, difficult and costly. If you can't readily answer these questions, don't worry. We will shortly. But if you don't answer these questions, you will not be able to attract significantly more customers.

Just as it is impossible to develop valid financial projections without an income statement, balance sheet, cash flow statement and assumptions, it is impossible to put together effective marketing and sales efforts without knowing the answers to these questions.

Let's take the sales funnel. Some call it a pipeline or pipeline report. It doesn't matter. What matters is learning the essence of what a sales funnel is, and more importantly, what *knowledge about the sales funnel* can do for your customer-attraction process.

Your sales funnel should look something like:

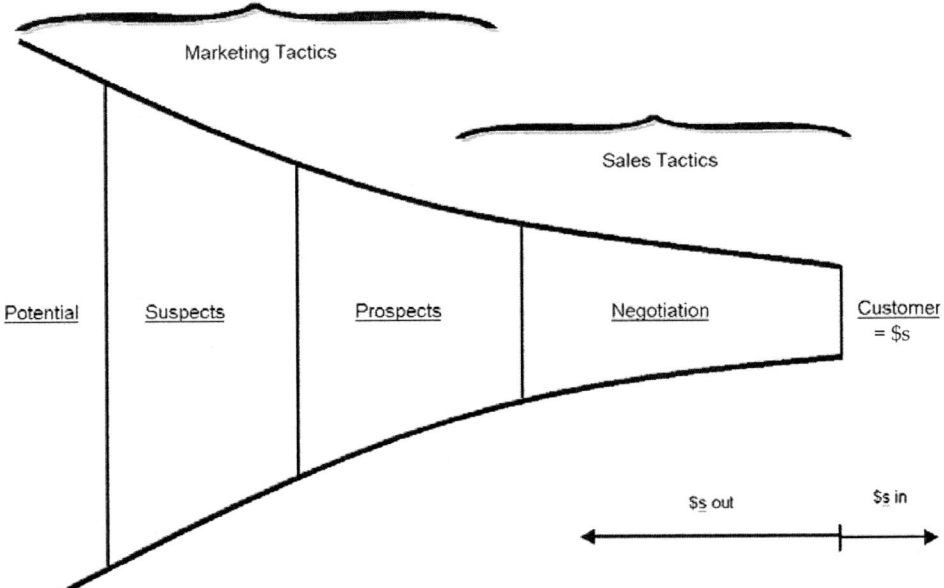

Some companies use far more partitions than the five shown above. (Act! uses eleven.) It doesn't matter: Whatever works for you. Simpler may be better, especially to start. How these terms are used in this book are:

Potential: People / organizations whose information (contact, characteristics) we *can* obtain.

Suspects: Prospective customers who have responded to initial marketing, or those organizations we feel need heightened / more focused marketing.

Prospects: Suspects who have passed our (& their) screening, who we feel might be good customers. Screening includes (1) understanding their needs and (2) they meet our "preferred customer" profile (more on this, later).

<u>Negotiation</u>: People / organizations we are talking with, one on one.

<u>Customer</u>: Book the sale and supply products &/or services!

The important thing about *having* a sales funnel is that it allows you to determine: [1] the difference between marketing and sales, [2] where in the funnel prospective customers may be, [3] what filters you apply in screening in, or out, prospective customers, and therefore [4] what your marketing tactics and sales tactics will be.

<u>The difference between marketing and sales</u>: Different people define these differently. One easy definition I use to tell the difference between marketing and sales is:

- Marketing = One to many
- Sales = One to one

One can argue with these definitions, and they may well be right. For purposes of attracting significantly more customers, we will be using these definitions. Mainly, so we can differentiate marketing and sales tactics, and how we'll be changing these tactics *after* we learn what we need to learn, via *strategic* marketing efforts.

Think about the marketing tactics you're using now. (You should have a list written up from the first Secret.) Many of these communicate one-to-many. Think about when you're talking with a potential customer: You are now squarely in sales mode. Not that you have to be a glad-handing "sales person". But you are in sales mode, trying to figure out how to get them to buy. Or, if you get into a Zen-like state of thinking, trying to figure out if they would benefit from your product or service. In any event, this difference will help you as you learn the highest-ROI tactics you can employ.

Where in the funnel are prospective customers: The longer a prospective customer is in the sales funnel, the more it costs you (to "market" to them), and the less profit you'll generate. So, it is essential that you know where they are in the funnel. Once you know where they are, you will be *able* to know what you should do. And you will also be able to start measuring the effectiveness (read: ROI) of your tactics.

Filters to apply in screening prospective customers, in or out: You probably have an excellent understanding of your products or services, but do you have an excellent understanding of who your (best) customers are, what they're buying (in their terms), and why they're buying? In order to attract significantly more customers – in good times and bad, you will need to know the answers to these questions, which we will get to in detail in the next chapter. In the mean time, it is important for you to have some idea, so you can create filters for your sales funnel. These filters include a definition of your preferred customer and the messages that resonate with them. Although we'll determine them in detail in the next chapter, we will need to make sure that we understand this a bit, here. That is – we need to apply filters in the sales funnel at the right point, to *reduce* our efforts and $s spent, *while* increasing the likelihood a prospective customer becomes an *actual* customer.

If, in our communications, we are able to allow someone to self-select out of our sales funnel, then we just saved everyone a bunch of time and money! If they will never be a great customer, why would we want to waste their time (and ours) trying to convince them to be our customer in the first place?

As we become more aware of the wasted of time, money and resources we use, this process starts looking pretty "green": Using fewer resources to accomplish even more is a good bet.

Think about Nordstrom's and Wal-Mart. I suspect their preferred customer profiles are quite different. In its simplest form, Nordstrom's want you to come in because you know you'll receive excellent service, an unparalleled return policy, extremely high quality and a pleasant shopping experience. You will be waited on.

Wal-Mart is the exact opposite. Which one is better? Depends on who you are as a shopper. And it *is* all about you, the shopper. It is not about their products and services. Do you want to be waited on, or do you want a great deal? You self-select. That means that Nordstrom's and Wal-Mart have done a great job communicating with you about themselves. You should do no less. Even when it's business to business.

<u>What your marketing tactics and sales tactics will be</u>: Once you *are able to* know what objectives and objections that prospective customers have, you will be able to move them through the funnel faster. Once you *learn what motivates them* to buy sooner, pay more, and tell all their business associates or friends, you will be able to adjust your marketing and sales tactics so that *they* speed through the funnel.

Less time in the funnel = more $s to your company!

Measure twice, cut once

By measuring where they are in the funnel, you'll be able to start measuring your "close ratios". If they get "stuck" in the Suspect area, you could improve your suspect-to-prospect close ratios. (How many prospective customers are suspects vs. how many were moved over to prospects.) You will also be able to measure your negotiation-to-customer close ratio. If it's too low, you know you're not negotiating very well. If it is easy, you may be leaving money on the table.

The important thing about *using* your sales funnel is, you can determine what is working and what is not working. Since you only have control over what you do, you can then improve (i.e., change) your behavior to higher-ROI tactics.

The most important thing about having and using a sales funnel is that you can realize the difference between marketing *tactics* and marketing *strategies*. Recall that marketing tactics are what you spend time and money on. A strategic view will help you learn *what* to spend your limited time and money on – that will yield the highest return on investment (ROI), *before* you spend a lot of time and money trying to figure it out – typically through trial and error.

Let's explore, further:

As long as a prospective customer is in the sales funnel, it will cost you time and money to either realize they will *never* be a great customer (and thus, reject them as soon as possible), or they will be a great customer, and figure out the most cost-effective way to get them through the funnel to become a paying customer. As soon as possible.

The great thing about this is that *you* get to decide who *you* think is a great customer! By doing so, you will free yourself from spending time and money on those companies and people who you should never "hire" as a customer in the first place!

All of the marketing and sales efforts that you implement to get suspects to become prospects (or reject), and then get prospects to negotiate (or reject), and then to become customers – are tactical. They are things you do. And they cost money. Most of the time, lots of it.

The question is not "How can we get the most prospective customers into our funnel?" It is "How can we get enough of the *right* prospective customers *through* our funnel." There is a big difference. In the first (tactical) case, you're thinking about getting in touch with as many suspects as possible, while in the second (strategic) case, you're thinking about who is the right prospective customer and how do we get them turbo-charged *through* the funnel –with the least effort (time & money) possible!

Remember: The longer prospective customers are in your sales funnel, the more it costs you to acquire them.

Again, if you take a Zen-like approach, instead of trying to be "opportunistic" (a euphemism for not knowing where to focus), you can spend as *little* as possible to define, then await the best possible customers. And by "await", I do not mean do nothing. I mean be open to the possibility that not every prospective customer is your best.

> During the middle of an engagement, someone at my client company (who signed about ten new customers a year) told me:
>
> "At a recent trade show where we presented, we found that hardly any of the thousand attendees had heard of us. We have been around for nearly ten years: every single one of those people should have known about us."
>
> My response: "If only 50 of those 1000 knew of you, and only 20 of those buy next year, your revenue would double."

My point: Get to those who are ready, willing and able to buy, *now*. Yes, you can plant seeds, build awareness, and generally spread out your marketing dollars (read tactics) along the awareness-to-call-to-action continuum. Most small businesses don't have the budget to do "all of the above". They are struggling. When the economy turns south (as it always does: it's called the business cycle, not the "new, or new-new economy"), focusing on generating *quality* revenue will yield enough higher-margin customers to be able to pay for awareness building. But first, you need to stay in business! In good times, and bad.

Another effect of focusing on those prospective customers, who could be your *best* customers, is – you get to shorten your sales cycle. Which boosts your revenue *rate*.

Let's get back to the internal assessment: measuring your current state of affairs, or corporate performance.

Major analyses you are going to do include: [1] Customers, [2] Prospective Customers (that did not buy), and [3] Marketing tactics. The best way to do these analyses is to use

Excel[tm]. If you are not familiar with Excel, find someone who is. Or – for a small fee – you can email a populated Excel spreadsheet to Synergy, and we will analyze it. (Go to Addendum #3: "How to Get Your Data Analyzed".)

In order to analyze your customer information, create a spreadsheet and list your customers, as well as some very important facts about them. This includes: Name, company, revenue generated to date, gross margin (after cost of goods), net profit (after other expenses), date of *first* contact, date of *first* contract (or order, or purchase), type of product or service purchased (if multiple, have columns for each), source for the lead (how did they *first* hear about you), time/effort & $s to market & sell each customer, and zip code (if consumer products).

There are several other areas you could list, but this is a good starting place. It will allow you to see how the process works and what value you can gain out of this. You will then be able to determine what other areas you'll need to assess.

Besides, you may not have access to *all* of the information listed above and might have it for *other* areas. The important thing is that you *learn the process*, so you can start keeping track of some very important customer-attraction data and learn how to assess its value: what it's telling you, so you can improve your marketing and sales tactics to generate 2x or 3x revenue - *while* (typically) spending less time and money.

Excel is a registered trademark of Microsoft.

An example of what this might look like:

#	Customer	Company	Revenue ($000)	Gross margin ($000)	Net profit ($000)	First Contact	First Contract	Product Type	Source	Effort to Close	Dollars to Close	Zip code
1	Joe P.	Company A	$10.0	$9.0	$3.15	01/01/06	01/01/07	Product A	Referral	32		97291
2	Tami R.	Company B	$25.0	$22.5	$7.88	02/01/07	02/12/07	Product C	Networking	16		98556
3	Jerry F.	Company C	$45.0	$40.5	$14.18	03/22/07	03/22/07	Product B	Trade Show	22	$5.0	85663
4	Denney C.	Company D	$5.0	$4.5	$1.58	04/02/06	04/01/07	Product C	Seminar	6		86542
5	Tamra B.	Company E	$120.0	$108.0	$37.80	05/02/06	05/15/07	Product B	Seminar	45		97229
6	Jorge J.	Company F	$15.0	$13.5	$4.73	02/04/07	06/08/07	Product C	Trade Show	2	$5.0	97006
7	Tim M.	Company G	$22.0	$19.8	$6.93	09/12/06	07/22/07	Product B	Networking	20		89101
8	Steve M.	Company H	$16.0	$14.4	$5.04	04/05/07	08/10/07	Service A	Referral	4		86222
9	Jeff W.	Company I	$96.0	$86.4	$30.24	09/04/06	09/01/07	Product B	Referral	3		55422
10	David R.	Company J	$45.0	$40.5	$14.18	09/19/07	10/19/07	Service A	Seminar	10		97035
11	Tony B.	Company K	$2.0	$1.8	$0.63	11/10/07	11/20/07	Product B	Referral	5		97229
12	Matt W.	Company L	$1.0	$0.9	$0.32	06/22/07	12/01/07	Service B	Seminar	12		97291
13	Josh F.	Company M	$6.0	$5.4	$1.89	09/18/06	01/15/07	Service C	Referral	10		97006
14	Steve B.	Company N	$6.0	$5.4	$1.89	08/10/06	02/01/07	Product B	Networking	5		97005
15	Eric J	Company O	$55.0	$49.5	$17.33	01/22/07	03/15/07	Product B	Networking	6		97006
16	Colette E.	Company P	$45.0	$40.5	$14.18	01/04/07	04/12/07	Service D	Referral	8		97229

Before we start building Prospective Customers and Marketing Tactics spreadsheets, let's look at the value that just one quick analysis can do for you. If you simply do a sort on Gross Revenue (highest to lowest), you will obtain this type of result:

#	Customer	Company	Revenue ($000)
5	Tamra B.	Company E	$120.0
9	Jeff W.	Company I	$96.0
15	Eric J	Company O	$55.0
3	Jerry F.	Company C	$45.0
10	David R.	Company J	$45.0
16	Colette E.	Company P	$45.0
2	Tami R.	Company B	$25.0
7	Tim M.	Company G	$22.0
8	Steve M.	Company H	$16.0
6	Jorge J.	Company F	$15.0
1	Joe P.	Company A	$10.0
13	Josh F.	Company M	$6.0
14	Steve B.	Company N	$6.0
4	Denney C.	Company D	$5.0
11	Tony B.	Company K	$2.0
12	Matt W.	Company L	$1.0

By doing a quick "Top 50% to Bottom 50%" analysis (next page), one finds that the top eight clients are worth $453,000, while the bottom eight clients are worth only $61,000. This represents a factor of over 7x! On a per-client basis, the top 8 account for $56,630 per client, whereas the bottom 8 account for $7,630 per client!

This looks like:

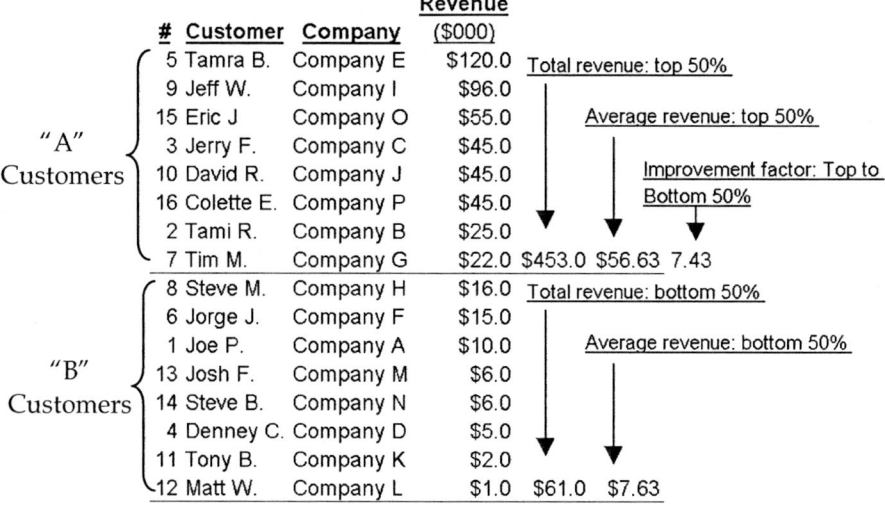

If it costs the same to acquire each customer, why would you spend any time on your "B" customers? (*If* you choose to call the bottom 50% "B" Customers. You may want to call your top 25% customers "A" and bottom 25% "D". It is up to you.)

In this example, the "potential maximum" increase in gross revenue – for the *same amount of marketing and sales efforts* – is over a factor of seven! If your company is generating $500,000, that equates to over $3.5 million. If it's $1 million, it would equate to $7.43 million! For the same marketing and sales effort!

At this point, it is important to recognize that by just doing the analysis your revenue will *not* magically increase. All this shows is that your revenue-potential is there. I want you to think in terms of "factors", not just percentages.

The power of this Secret is to show you that – with the *right* marketing and sales tactics – you have the potential to generate *significantly* more revenue. Chances are, you will not be able to squeeze out this type of performance. But even if you fail to meet a 7x improvement, and only get to 2x, that's still *two times your current revenue*!

It all has to do with KNOWING the facts and making decisions based on these facts. Not assuming anything. Being open to change. And learning what it is *you* need to know to change your marketing and sales tactics – to attract significantly more "A" customers. In terrible times and great times.

Before we do more analyses, I want to share what the return on investment (ROI) improvements can mean for you. I have applied this process to 14 Synergy clients, and have achieved the following improvements in ROI:

Client	ROI (factor)
Assignment #1	40.0 x
Assignment #2	7.3 x
Assignment #3	350.0 x
Assignment #4	80.0 x
Assignment #5	50.0 x
Assignment #6	9.3 x
Assignment #7	333.0 x
Assignment #8	7.0 x
Assignment #9	250.0 x
Assignment #10	10.0 x
Assignment #11	6.7 x
Assignment #12	220.0 x
Assignment #13	12.5 x
Assignment #14	40.0 x
Average	101.1 x
Median	40.0 x

Note: In this case, ROI means the improvement factor (multiplier) that my clients realized by using all of these secrets.

> Results vary according to the specifics of the company, market, niche, products, customers, geographic region, etc. Although there is no way to predict the outcome of new marketing & sales tactics implemented as a result of these analyses, you can be sure that you will be able to attract significantly more customers. And by *not* doing these analyses, you can not *know* how to optimize your tactics. If you did, you probably would not have purchased this book. ☺

Let's look at a couple more analyses, and what the answers can do for you: viewing customers through your product / service lens. This means sorting on the Product and/or Service types. Performing a quick Pareto analysis* on the Products and Services shows that this company should be focusing their outbound marketing & sales efforts on Product B. Certainly, accepting orders for the others, but putting their limited *outbound* marketing resources on Product B.

From just a simple sort on the products and services:

#	Customer	Company	Revenue ($000)	Product Type	
1	Joe P.	Company A	$10.0	Product A	$10.0
3	Jerry F.	Company C	$45.0	Product B	
5	Tamra B.	Company E	$120.0	Product B	
7	Tim M.	Company G	$22.0	Product B	
9	Jeff W.	Company I	$96.0	Product B	
11	Tony B.	Company K	$2.0	Product B	
14	Steve B.	Company N	$6.0	Product B	
15	Eric J	Company O	$55.0	Product B	$346.0
2	Tami R.	Company B	$25.0	Product C	
4	Denney C.	Company D	$5.0	Product C	
6	Jorge J.	Company F	$15.0	Product C	$45.0
8	Steve M.	Company H	$16.0	Service A	
10	David R.	Company J	$45.0	Service A	$62.0
12	Matt W.	Company L	$1.0	Service B	$1.0
13	Josh F.	Company M	$6.0	Service C	$6.0
16	Colette E.	Company P	$45.0	Service D	$45.0

* Google the phrase "Pareto analysis" if you haven't heard of it.

Rearranging these numbers, so that we better understand the Products and Services yields:

	Revenue	# of items	Revenue / item
Product A	$10.0	1	$10.0
Product B	$346.0	7	$49.4
Product C	$45.0	3	$15.0
Service A	$62.0	2	$31.0
Service B	$1.0	1	$1.0
Service C	$6.0	1	$6.0
Service D	$45.0	1	$45.0

Not only does Product B bring in the most money (over 5 times the next-highest item), but it also yields the highest per-sale revenue. If all products sold were "B", another $271K would have been generated. (Left to the reader to determine.)

By performing another quick analysis, we find that the top 3 products and services also outperform the bottom 4 products and services by a 5 to 1 margin:

	Revenue	# of items	Revenue / item	Ave. for group	Factor
Product B	$0.0	7	$49.4		
Service D	$0.0	1	$45.0		
Service A	$0.0	2	$31.0	$41.8	5.2 x
Product C	$0.0	3	$15.0		
Product A	$45.0	1	$10.0		
Service C	$0.0	1	$6.0		
Service B	$0.0	1	$1.0	$8.0	

With just a couple of "internal assessments" you now know your best customers, products and services.

Now, let's look at sales cycle. By subtracting the "date of first *contract*" from "date of first *contact*", you can determine the number of days, which is the sales cycle for these 16 clients.

From this, simply averaging the number of days will tell you the average sales cycle is 5 months. This may be a long cycle or short – depending on your industry, products, location, etc. But it is a metric against which you can measure future performance.

#	Customer	Company	First Contact	First Contract	Days to Close
1	Joe P.	Company A	01/01/06	01/01/07	365
2	Tami R.	Company B	02/01/07	02/12/07	11
3	Jerry F.	Company C	03/22/07	03/22/07	0
4	Denney C.	Company D	04/02/06	04/01/07	364
5	Tamra B.	Company E	05/02/06	05/15/07	378
6	Jorge J.	Company F	02/04/07	06/08/07	124
7	Tim M.	Company G	09/12/06	07/22/07	313
8	Steve M.	Company H	04/05/07	08/10/07	127
9	Jeff W.	Company I	09/04/06	09/01/07	362
10	David R.	Company J	09/19/07	10/19/07	30
11	Tony B.	Company K	11/10/07	11/20/07	10
12	Matt W.	Company L	06/22/07	12/01/07	162
13	Josh F.	Company M	09/18/06	01/15/07	119
14	Steve B.	Company N	08/10/06	02/01/07	175
15	Eric J	Company O	01/22/07	03/15/07	52
16	Colette E.	Company P	01/04/07	04/12/07	98
				Average days to close:	168
				Average months to close:	5

In the next chapter, we will find out how to dramatically shorten your sales cycle. At least now, with an internal assessment, you'll know what it is!

Let's assess how you think your current customers heard about you; This would be the source of the lead. I bet you know what's coming up. Sorting on the source:

#	Customer	Company	Revenue ($000)	Source	
2	Tami R.	Company B	$25.0	Networking	
7	Tim M.	Company G	$22.0	Networking	
14	Steve B.	Company N	$6.0	Networking	
15	Eric J	Company O	$55.0	Networking	$108.0
1	Joe P.	Company A	$10.0	Referral	
8	Steve M.	Company H	$16.0	Referral	
9	Jeff W.	Company I	$96.0	Referral	
11	Tony B.	Company K	$2.0	Referral	
13	Josh F.	Company M	$6.0	Referral	
16	Colette E.	Company P	$45.0	Referral	$175.0
4	Denney C.	Company D	$5.0	Seminar	
5	Tamra B.	Company E	$120.0	Seminar	
10	David R.	Company J	$45.0	Seminar	
12	Matt W.	Company L	$1.0	Seminar	$171.0
3	Jerry F.	Company C	$45.0	Trade Show	
6	Jorge J.	Company F	$15.0	Trade Show	$60.0

From here, we'll compile the results as a function of "Source":

Source	Revenue ($000)		
Referral	$175.0	292%	($175 / $60 = 292%)
Seminar	$171.0		
Networking	$108.0		
Trade Show	$60.0		

From this analysis, you can see that referrals provide 292% improvement in revenue over Trade Shows. At this point, we are just gathering data, turning it into information, so we can gain knowledge. Resist making snap decisions on this (like stopping all trade shows). Your ability to make even better decisions (based on validating your internal assessment results) will come after performing *external* assessments.

There are many more assessments you can perform and insights you can gain.

We are going to perform one more analysis to show the intense value that this Secret can provide you.

Let's take a look at one type of profitability. That is – what is the cost to acquire one customer and what is the value of one customer? Wouldn't this be nice to know? With this information, we should be able to focus on our best (i.e., "A") prospective customers.

In order to proceed, you will need to determine what your hourly rate is. Or, what it should be. Of course, it depends on the size of your company, its profitability, and many other variables. Since you are the CEO, perhaps your value should be in the $100 to $500 per hour, or more. Even if your check doesn't reflect this. Let's assume $175 per hour.

I am taking some liberties with the numbers in the case we are examining to illustrate my point. (If you have a financial background, please stick with me until we work through it.)

If you spend $20,000 on each trade show and $5,000 on each seminar you put on, and we take into account the time you spend negotiating with each customer, we find that:

- The top 8 customers provide *52 times* more "profit" than the bottom 8 customers do.
- The top four provide 66x the bottom 8 (analysis left to you).
- The bottom 4 customers are costing you money!

The following table shows how to arrive at these conclusions:

#	Customer	Company	Gross margin ($000)	Effort to Close	Dollars to Close	Total Costs	Prof/Loss		
5	Tamra B.	Company E	$108.0	45	$5.0	$7.9	$96.3		
9	Jeff W.	Company I	$86.4	20		$3.5	$83.4		
15	Eric J	Company O	$49.5	20		$3.5	$46.5		
16	Colette E.	Company P	$40.5	20		$3.5	$37.5		
10	David R.	Company J	$40.5	10	$5.0	$1.8	$34.0		
2	Tami R.	Company B	$22.5	16		$2.8	$20.1		
3	Jerry F.	Company C	$40.5	22	$20.0	$3.9	$17.2		
7	Tim M.	Company G	$19.8	20		$3.5	$16.8	351.75	52 x
8	Steve M.	Company H	$14.4	20		$3.5	$11.4		
14	Steve B.	Company N	$5.4	5		$0.9	$4.7		
1	Joe P.	Company A	$9.0	32		$5.6	$4.2		
13	Josh F.	Company M	$5.4	10		$1.8	$3.9		
11	Tony B.	Company K	$1.8	20		$3.5	-$1.2		
4	Denney C.	Company D	$4.5	20	$5.0	$3.5	-$3.5		
12	Matt W.	Company L	$0.9	12	$5.0	$2.1	-$5.9		
6	Jorge J.	Company F	$13.5	2	$20.0	$0.4	-$6.8	6.75	

There are several more analyses you can do, depending on the data you maintain. Each can provide you with information to make significantly better decisions, which can yield significantly more customers.

Now, let's get to those other two areas: Prospective Customers (who did not buy), and Marketing Tactics.

Prospective Customers

For Prospective Customers, list all who did not buy. If you own a consumer or retail company and do not have this kind of information, start asking for this kind of information. Incentivize your prospects to share it with you. You will see why the information you could gain is golden. Once you list your "lost" customers, make sure you include why they didn't buy. Also include what the sale could have been and what products and services you were offering.

If you sort on why they did not buy, you will gain insights into *how much each reason is costing you*. (Use the same sorting / Pareto assessment as we did earlier.) Once you have this information, you will be able to make better decisions on how you can overcome objections.

If the major reason is that you are not offering the right product or service, and it is costing you more (in lost revenue) than you are currently making, you have a choice to make. Offer the service, or find someone who can, where you can generate referral fees, or some other way to monetize your efforts.

If the major reason is that you're difficult to do business with, or have a lengthy proposal process or your products do not align with your marketing messages; these are all things you can *do* something about.

We cannot change prospective customers, but we can change the way we approach them, screen them (in or out), talk with them, and engage them. We only have control over our own actions, so let's find out what *we* need to change!

Another key benefit of learning why your prospective customers did not buy, is that you know *where in the sales funnel* they are jettisoning out. Once you know this, you can take action to change *what you are doing* at that point. (From Suspect to Prospect, or from Prospect to Negotiation, or from Negotiation to Closing business.)

Marketing Tactics

By simply determining how you are currently spending money, you will be able to calculate your return on investment.

An example of a client's marketing expenses each year:

Marketing Tactic	Expenses
PR	$ 77,400
Trade Magazine Advertising	$ 43,500
Referral / Testimonials	$ 1,000
Web / SEO	$ 24,250
Trade Shows	$ 9,250
Direct Vendor Contacts	$ 6,000
	$ 161,400

If revenue is associated with each marketing tactic, you will see the value of each marketing method:

Marketing Tactic	Expenses	Gross Revenue	Simple ROI
PR	$ 77,400	$ 4,000	0.05X
Trade Magazine Advertising	$ 43,500	$ 2,000	0.05X
Referral / Testimonials	$ 1,000	$ 250,000	250.00X
Web / SEO	$ 24,250	$ 80,000	3.30X
Trade Shows	$ 9,250	$ 10,000	1.08X
Direct Vendor Contacts	$ 6,000	$ 45,000	7.50X
	$ 161,400	$ 160,400	2.40X

Clearly, referrals / testimonials provide the highest-ROI, while the area of highest expense (Trade Magazine Advertising) provides the lowest ROI. What would you do if this were your company? I would pocket ½ of the $120K* and spend the other half on developing some sort of referral award program!

* $120K = $77K + 43K

This process works for consumer-oriented companies and business-to-business companies

The principles presented in this book apply to companies with either consumers or business customers. You may need to extrapolate a bit. For instance the "negotiation" might just be for the 20 seconds they look at a price in your retail store – and decide to buy, or not.

This process works for start-up companies, too

If your company is in start-up mode, in order to move forward you will *have* to make some assumption about who your best customers will be – for a while. However, knowing they are assumptions, and then working towards validating them or replacing them with the facts (by implementing the next Secret) will help you attract significantly more customers – in good times and bad.

Secret #6
Ask your customers / prospects what you need to know

Now that you have your baseline assessment of your preferred customer, how they found you, how much it cost to acquire them, the value they are to you, how long it took, why some said no, and the effectiveness of your marketing, you are ready to talk with your customers. Or prospective customers, if you currently have none.

Just as you will be able to make great decisions based on great information* about your company, in order to attract significantly more "A" customers, you will need to learn more about your customers and prospects than you ever have before.

Before we get started, I want you to get a pen and paper, and write down your answers to the following question. Again, you will only gain insights if you actually stop and do this exercise. So, please take the time to jot down your thoughts:

When you are looking to attract and close customers, what do you need to know?

---

* "How to Predict the Future"; from *The Entrepreneur's Survival Guide*, ISBN 0-9708665-2-6.

Please take your time and brainstorm as many things as you need to know – in order to "close" customers.

If you are like most of the CEOs in my seminars who answer this question in the following ways, you are in good company. Most provide these ideas:

- What is your budget?
- Time frame for a decision?
- Am I on the right track?
- Any competitors?
- Do you have any objections?
- What keeps you awake at night?
- What's working? What's not working?
- Who are *your* customers?
- Any roadblocks to success
- Roadblocks to moving forward?
- What are your goals?
- What are your challenges?
- If I were to overcome your objections to your satisfaction, would you want to move forward with purchasing our solution?

These are great questions, when you are selling. They provide insights into our prospective customers' minds, and they help you relate with their issues and concerns.

However, these are tactical sales questions, not strategies.

The question is thus: *"What do you need to know in order to attract significantly more customers?"*

Before we answer this question, let's take a deep breath and think back to the beginning of this book: Only after you learn and implement Secrets # 2, 3, & 4, will Secret #6 be of any value to you. What are those secrets again? [#2] Be 100% open to change. [#3] Assume nothing. [#4] Recognize you may need to learn a new language.

The reason for these prior secrets is – through asking your customers what *you* need to know – you will be presented with potentially business-altering information. If you are not open to hearing it, make assumptions about what it means, and/or are not ready to learn a new language, none of this matters. You will gain nothing by just reading this book.

You are now ready.

You will need to know four things to attract significantly more customers. And if you get the answers (really) right, this is *all* you will need to know, to finish your strategic-level assessment. You need to know:

- <u>Who</u> are your best customers? ("A" customers)
- <u>What</u> are they buying? (Tangible: benefits & features)
- <u>Why</u> are they buying? (Intangible: personal motivation)
- <u>How</u> do they make a buying decision? (Decision process)

The reason we want to know the answers to these four questions is because we want to learn their language. The "Who" provides us the *Market*. The "What" and "Why" will yield the highest-ROI *Message*(s), and the "How" will tell us exactly how to best reach our preferred customers; your *Method*.

Once you *know* the answers to these questions, you will be well on your way to making superior decisions about your marketing and sales tactics. You will no longer waste money on efforts that don't work. You will no longer chase prospective customers who don't fit your profile. Your sales cycle will shrink. Average sales per customer will increase. Your cost of acquiring customers will decrease. Your profitability will increase. You will have more time on your hands for things you enjoy. And it will likely cost you far less for your marketing and sales efforts.

Who are your best customers?

At this point, you have some homework to do. Whether you've been in business 6 months or 6 years, you have a good gut feel (read: assumption) as to who your best customers are. Now that you've performed the internal assessment (discussed in the previous chapter), you have a much *better* understanding of who your preferred customers are. In fact, take some time to write down your Preferred Customer Profile. Why? Because if you don't know, or can't communicate succinctly with anyone else about who you can really help, how will they know they could be a customer? Or refer others to you?

Based on your gut feel, along with the top 25% to 50% of the customers identified in your Internal Assessment, figure out "What is it about those customers that make them so good for my business?" Jot down your thoughts, and over time, you will continue updating your profile until it really rings true – about your *best* customers.

Preferred Customer Profile: This needs to be simple and no more than one page. (For an example, go to www.synergy-usa.com/PreferredClientProfile.pdf) At this point, you will probably have your assumptions built in. As long as you recognize you will be learning more as you perform the external assessment and that your assumed profile may well change, you will be fine.

Please take the time to write it down, before reading further.

We want to talk with your best customers, not your worst. We don't care to attract more of those! Just the best ones. So, when we perform customer research (not market research), we need to know enough about their attributes, so we'll ask about those. For example:

- For a consumer (ex: retail) company: if the average revenue in one zip code is 5x the average in another, let's go to the better-performing zip code!
- For a wholesale company, if mid-sized companies pay up-front and ease your cash-flow, let's talk with them.

What are they buying? (Tangible: benefits & features)

You may have heard the saying "Sell benefits, not features". Although this is an important distinction, both benefits and features really get at the "what". Certainly, benefits answer the question "What's in it for me?" – from the prospective customers' perspective.

Questions you want to know the answers to include: What tangible attributes do they want? Are they buying your products and services because they are faster? Smaller? More durable? Integrated? Easily changed?

By answering these questions, you will be able to learn which of your offerings' features to discuss with prospects. If there are 25 features, and your prospects are only interested in five, then why spend any time discussing the other twenty? This is where you start learning their exact language. Sometimes a one-word change in your message can make a significant difference!

Why are they buying? (Intangible: personal motivation)

Understanding the benefits enjoyed by customers of your product or service is important. But it only addresses one aspect of the whole buying experience. Even more important than answering the "benefit" question, is to learn their *fundamental reasons for buying*, in the first place.

> Consider an information technology (IT) solution that is sold to Fortune 1000 companies. Who probably makes the buying decision? Although everyone will tell you "the team", in many cases it may actually be the CFO. If you are selling on features, then you will talk about (for example) "the ability to keep track of time, per product line , per person, per vendor, all matrixed together, with online & real-time reporting", etc. etc. If you are selling on benefits, you may discuss the results of keeping track of time, per product line, etc… in terms of the value it provides the prospect's company. Something like "This solution identifies and frees up an average of $50,000 within the first six months." Much more powerful than trying to sell "a thing that does stuff".
>
> It is an interesting side note that CFOs' average tenure at Fortune 1000 companies is between a year and a half to four years. The true motivation for the CFO's decision may have nothing to do with features, or benefits. It has to do with the CFO keeping their job.
>
> The sales person who knows that this is the true motivation (because you, the strategic-thinking CEO decided to perform the necessary research to find out the "Why?" to support your sales team), will get the sale over someone selling features and even benefits.

How do they make a buying decision? (Decision process)

Once you analyze your company's performance, you will be quite far along in learning how your customers buy. Please recognize that just because your current customers buy a certain way, doesn't mean your preferred customers will. Through an assessment of your customers and prospective customers, you will be able validate your "internal" findings.

If everyone in your business-to-business industry is presenting at trade shows, but your customers buy because of referrals, why go to trade shows? If coupons overwhelmingly bring consumers to your retail store, why advertise in the yellow pages? The methods you *like* to use may have worked in the past, but times change. And they're changing rapidly. A much more effective way is to learn before you spend money on low-return methods. And the best way to do that is to statistically learn your customers' preferred methods.

I use the terms "specific" and "statistically" for each of these four areas. The reason is to avoid the "loudest, last customer" syndrome. You know… that one customer or prospect who was/is insistent that you do this or that… while nine out of ten others quietly prefer something else. If you don't uncover the hidden majority-driven preferences, you will be forever lagging in sales.

Let's assume you have asked your customers how they make their buying decision, and eight ways (methods) were mentioned:

- Advertising
- Brochures
- Catalogs
- Newsletters
- PR
- Seminars
- Trade Shows
- Web searches

At first glance, it may seem that the best approach is to take your "marketing dollar" or "marketing hour" (both, limited resources) and cut them up into eight pieces and apply equally in these eight areas. That glance would be wrong. Especially in light of the information we gathered on each method (read "tactic"). What if our customer research showed the following customer responses to these tactics:

#	Method	# mentioned	% mentioned
1	Seminars	44	31%
2	PR	22	16%
3	Advertising	20	14%
4	Catalogs	19	14%
5	Web searches	13	9%
6	Newsletters	12	9%
7	Brochures	8	6%
8	Trade Shows	2	1%
		140	100%

Plotting these results would look like:

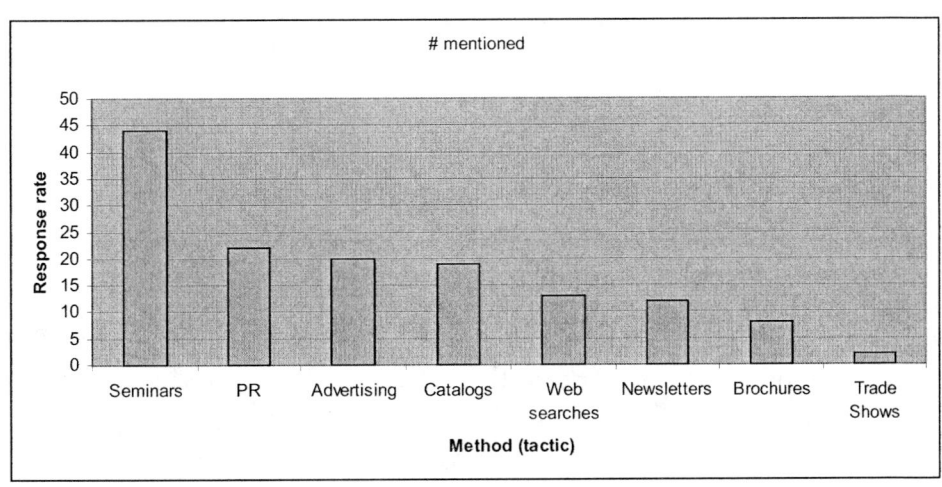

The easy conclusion is – if Seminars are used by a two to one margin in making a decision to buy your product, why would you spend a dime on trade shows?

Yet, this is precisely what companies do. In fact, without this type of information, companies regularly hire marketing firms to determine how they can improve their advertising response rates. Why? Why bother spending more money or putting your money down a rat-hole, trying to make advertising better when it is the third-best approach? Doubling ad performance is *still* less productive than seminars already are! And with seminars, you only need to make it 10% better to equal a 50% improvement in advertising response rates.

In your case, perhaps advertising is the best thing to do. You'll have to perform the research to *know*.

Continuing to spend money in areas without the highest ROI is madness. Yet, companies do it all the time.

We could put together the same type of chart to address the Message (once we have answers from the What and Why questions). If there is a number one message that resonates with prospective customers, we may well get the same relative response rates. Why put *any other* message in our marketing?

I performed this assessment on my own consultancy (after 13 years in business, having done it for several others before that: Dentists don't work on their own teeth). I found out that my preferred customers (CEOs) want to attract more customers as their number one objective. This continues to be the top message when I survey different industries, sizes of companies, etc. So my outbound efforts use this message. Because it resonates!

If a VP of Marketing hires me, they may want me to make their trade shows better. I don't do that! Plenty of other companies do, and do it well. I help CEOs figure out *if* they should even be going to trade shows. That is where the intense value of performing this process can be found.

> I had one client who regularly spent $10,000 per month on advertising. When I performed the external research, exactly 0% of my client's customers said they made buying decisions because of his advertising. My client immediately cut all advertising and saved $120,000 per year! It didn't even cost him a quarter of that much to find out what he should do. In nine year's time (how long they had been in business), this equates to over $1 million in savings.
>
> This same client's average sales cycle was 7.5 months (determined through an internal assessment: Secret #5). Once I determined (through customer research: Secret #6) that the best method to reach their customers was with seminars – where my client helped his prospective customers understand how to identify and overcome a particularly difficult problem – the average sales cycle was determined to be only 2 months. This represents a 73% sales cycle reduction.

Thank goodness my client was open to learning and checked his assumptions at the door.

How do you do this for *your* company? Although this process and these secrets are applicable to any company -- of any size, you *must* ask the right questions, that are right for your company, your customers, your market, your products and services.

The trick to know what questions to ask, to get at the essence of these over-arching four questions (who, what, why, and how). It is not just by asking these four questions straight up. I've had CEOs "pick my brain" then try it themselves, without the success others (my clients) have enjoyed, because there is more than meets the eye. They think it will be "easy street" for them.

Assessment process to overcome your assumptions

If you're looking to obtain as much information about your prospective customers as possible, you will need to ask your best customers and who you think are best-fit prospective customers (based on your preferred customer profile) to take a brief survey, and analyze it appropriately. (It needs to be brief: 15 to 25 questions [maximum], 5 to 10 minutes [maximum].) You can use a paper survey (two pages maximum), or a web-based solution, like Zoomerang.com. You will also need to reach them in a way that maximizes their response rates.

Anything you do in your survey process needs be geared towards two things: [1] getting at the essence of the information *you need*, and [2] making it easy to obtain responses.

A quick word on the number of responses you need: For the purposes of figuring out how to attract significantly more customers, and with the analysis process explained later, you may need only 15 or so responses. Not the hundreds that some firms want you to have. Yes, more is better, and too few can be disastrous. Especially if what you conclude is exactly wrong. But the process takes care of this, with far fewer respondents. (Please see Addendum #1 for real-world examples, including one engagement where, with only 17 respondents – when integrated with the rest of the secrets – provided enough information to increase the value of a client company from $1 million (prior acquisition offer) to an actual $17 million acquisition, including cash, stock and earn-out.) Just recognize that serious statistical errors exist with few responses.

A summary of the patent-pending process is listed below, with details to follow:

1) Determine / define your preferred customer profile.
2) Develop list of current customers/prospective customers.
3) Create a cover letter / outgoing email.
4) Offer something of value (stated in the letter/email).
5) Develop the survey.
6) Send out the letters / emails to your list.
7) Wait for responses.
8) Analyze responses.
9) Draw logical conclusions.
10) Change your marketing and sales behavior accordingly.

Each of these steps is discussed in further detail, below:

1) <u>Determine / define your preferred customer profile</u>: This was covered earlier.

2) <u>Develop a list of current customers and prospective customers</u> who you think match this profile. Include their contact information, both email and snail-mail. If they are prospective customers, take the time to review their website or find out if they fit your preferred customer profile.

3) <u>Create a cover letter / outgoing email</u> that explains what you are doing (research), why you are doing it (to learn

to serve customers better), and how it will help you help them (provide even better solutions). Make sure they are individualized: This is not a blanket mailing. More personal = higher response rates.

4) <u>Offer something of value</u> (stated in the letter/email: to increase response rates): I have tried *many* things, and the best is consumer electronics. Something they might not buy for themselves, but want. Or they might give someone they know. Like a Garmin eTrex Handheld GPS. It's abut $100 and will be the best $100 you spend.

5) <u>Develop the survey</u>. Have others read it, take it and that it takes less than 5 to 10 minutes. More on this later.

6) <u>Send out the letters / emails</u> (#3, above) to your list (#2, above), *containing* the survey (if via letter) or *linked to* the survey (if via email). If you send a letter, hand-write the address and use a stamp, not a postage machine. Include a self-addressed, stamped envelope to make it easy for them to return the survey. If you send an email, make sure that each one is individually addressed. No spam!

7) <u>Wait for responses</u>. This may be a couple days, or you may find you receive no responses. If the email and survey are brief, well-written, and you have some sort of prior relationship with the individual, the response rate can be as high as 25%. I've had as high as 50%. And as low as 0%. If after a week you have received no responses, you will need to get creative. Rarely has it taken more than a second approach to gain enough responses to draw valid conclusions. However, in one case I had to try eleven different methods to obtain responses.

8) <u>Analyze responses</u>: The analyses you use are a function of the information you want and the survey style you use. More on this, in a bit.

9) <u>Draw logical conclusions</u>: Once you have performed the analyses, take a look at the knowledge you've gained. Invite others on your team to review the assessment and come to some conclusions about what you should do differently – to get different results.

10) <u>Change your marketing and sales behavior accordingly</u>: This process is for naught if you are not going to *do* something about what you've just learned. Your marketing team may be excellent at implementation, and *now* you know what needs to be implemented. As Nike says: "Just Do It!".

Developing your survey to find out what *you* need to know

Remember that you want answers to four questions:

> *Who* is buying?   *What* are they buying?
> *Why* are they buying?   *How* do they buy?

Unfortunately, you can't just ask these four questions and then be done with it. You will have to set the stage, use some techniques that will you help you get at the *essence* of their thinking (through their answers), and be able to sift through the noise you are about to receive.

You will need to ask open-ended questions and closed-ended questions to learn the information you need.

Note: In the context of customer research, I am defining "open-ended" as a question where they can answer anything they want, for as long as they want. Many will just put in a word or three. Others will write a paragraph. In the analysis process (later), we'll learn how to deal with these responses, taking qualitative information and turning it into quantitative information, upon which you can make important decisions, with far-reaching (positive) effects.

I am defining "closed-ended" questions as those where you will provide a list of answers that are either one-choice-only, or where they can select multiple answers, or can rate each choice along a range you have defined. Market-research firms may beg to differ on these definitions.

Who is buying?

As discussed earlier, if your customers are consumers, perhaps zip codes are important to know. As is age, income and profession. You might want to hold off asking these questions (question-order in the survey) until you have established a bit of a relationship through less-intrusive questions. If your customers are businesses, then it is appropriate to learn who, within the company makes buying decisions. For instance, if CFOs make the decisions, why are you trying to sell to a controller, or president? Doing so will lengthen your sales cycle. Therefore, job title may be important.

Every situation, industry, market niche, product, service, location, etc. is different – so you will need to develop the right questions for your situation, or hire someone who has done this many times.

What are they buying?

We are trying to understand *their* perspective of what they are buying. It is important to learn *their* language – in how they describe your product or service. Why? Because we need to get into *their way of thinking* if we are to resonate with them and *speak* their language. If they call something a "protocol" and you like the term "process", they will buy from someone who calls it a protocol. If it's "product development" instead of "project management" or "integrated software" instead of "compact software", then speak to prospective customers in *their* language.

Why are they buying?

The real trick is learning their fundamental motivation for making a purchase. You may have heard the phrase "Sell the sizzle, not the steak." Although this is correct, you can turbo-charge your customer-attraction process (and beat your competitors who are still in the "benefits" frame of mind), by taking it one step further. (Recall the earlier story about the CFO, and why they may make decisions?)

By learning why they buy, you may shorten your sales cycle.

> I was meeting with the COO of a small start-up who told me their customers have a "19 month sales cycle". They had been in business for 19 months and had yet to make a sale. With this two-minute exchange, I was able to determine they had not yet uncovered their prospects' underlying motivation.

> I did not get the consulting assignment because the COO was not open to learning another language, and had made (and invested in) his assumption about the sales cycle as the reason they weren't performing (closing deals). Wrong.
>
> They went out of business within another few months.

The book "Ready, Fire, Aim" by Michael Masterson provides an excellent perspective on how to overcome these challenges.

<u>How are they buying?</u>

If your customers are buying 50% of their annual purchases during trade shows, you'd better go to trade shows. If 80% of people buy because they taste your product, you'd better provide samples.

Resist the urge to just use closed-ended questions. Some of my clients want to do that when they review the survey for the first time. What makes us think we are all-knowing? Open-ended questions allow customers and prospects to provide insights that we might not have. Be sure to ask these before the closed-ended versions.

Analyzing responses: To learn what *you* need to know to attract significantly more customers

Although there are several analysis methodologies you can perform, two basic methods will serve you well. One is for closed-ended questions and the second is for open-ended questions. Recall that the main goal of the analysis is to turn data into information, so that you can make great decisions that generate results. Therefore, you will want to get the most you can out of the limited responses you receive.

Closed-ended questions: Analysis process

The easiest analysis to perform is to simply develop a graphic that shows what percentage of respondents selected a choice. An example is shown, below. (This is a Zoomerang screen shot.) What conclusion would you draw from these results?

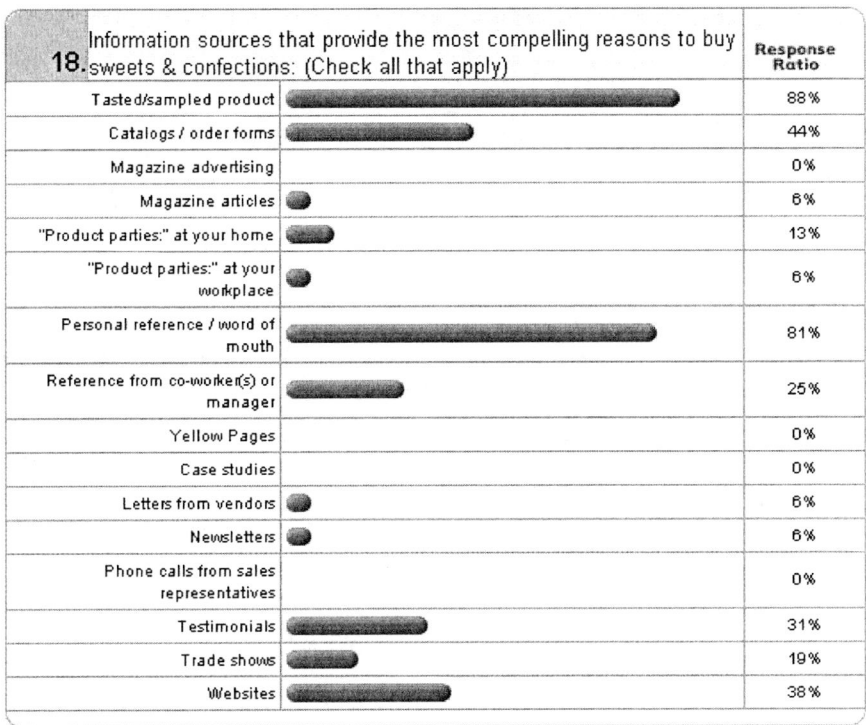

18. Information sources that provide the most compelling reasons to buy sweets & confections: (Check all that apply)	Response Ratio
Tasted/sampled product	88%
Catalogs / order forms	44%
Magazine advertising	0%
Magazine articles	6%
"Product parties:" at your home	13%
"Product parties:" at your workplace	6%
Personal reference / word of mouth	81%
Reference from co-worker(s) or manager	25%
Yellow Pages	0%
Case studies	0%
Letters from vendors	6%
Newsletters	6%
Phone calls from sales representatives	0%
Testimonials	31%
Trade shows	19%
Websites	38%

For a rating type of question (rate each item below, 1 – 7), the graphic on the following page could be developed. (A competitive positioning analysis was needed in this case.) What conclusions would you draw from these results?

When you look at the raw data you would see that Something Sweeeet had over 3x times, in percentage terms (and six times as many people) rating in the "Wow!" factor, over the number of people who rated Moonstruck's in that factor. This is significant. (For clarity, the # of respondents are not shown.)

28. If you've heard of the following companies, please let us know what you think. We would like to know what you think of each company's product QUALITY (taste, value, packaging, etc.):							
The top percentage indicates total respondent ratio; the bottom number represents actual number of respondents selecting the option	1 Terrible	2 Just	3 Decent	4 Pretty good	5 Great	6 Excellent!	7 Wow! / Unbelievable!
1. Candy Basket	0%	25%	25%	0%	25%	25%	0%
2. Cookie Bouquet	0%	17%	50%	33%	0%	0%	0%
3. Harry & David's	0%	0%	29%	36%	14%	21%	0%
4. Marsee Baking	0%	0%	25%	50%	25%	0%	0%
5. Moonstruck Chocolates	0%	0%	0%	0%	50%	38%	13%
6. Mrs. Fields	11%	22%	11%	11%	22%	22%	0%
7. See's Candies	0%	7%	0%	27%	33%	33%	0%
8. Something Sweeeet	0%	0%	0%	7%	0%	50%	43%
9. Virtual Chocolate	0%	0%	100%	0%	0%	0%	0%

Open-ended questions: Analysis process

The trick with analyzing answers to open-ended questions is to convert *qualitative* information into *quantitative* information. Answers may appear totally random. Or you may spot a recurring theme, and be able to draw specific conclusions from the responses.

Let's start with an example where we asked Chief Information Officers (CIOs) "*What business needs do your current IT projects address?*" The responses were a compendium of a whole host of business needs. To make my point, they are included on the next page:

Project management, available skills, requirements, Too few people for everything that needs to get done, ever-increasingly complex technology, unsure of which competing technology to use. Backup/Infrastructure Web Development Database Structure, Security, -Development Architecture, -Keeping current with new releases before vendors drop support Maintaining high levels of support for our customers. Choosing to adapt new technologies that truly have business benefit. Sarbanes Oxley compliance. Establishment of Project Management Office Collaboration with third-parties Demand versus willingness to pay Finding top quality consultants Decrease in work available/Increased competition Sarbanes Oxley compliance. Merging instances of JDE. End User reporting. Business Intelligence, corporate wide standardization of change management and SDLC, Security and virus protection Wireless technologies Licensing costs, Integration Acquisitions Supporting multiple systems Implementing enterprise apps, security, administration, costs, Managing Executive Management team to provide resources and funding to meet the needs of the business, Compliance with Sarbanes Oxley Act of 2002, and meeting the needs of the 404 audit in 2005, Gaining end user commitment and ownership of projects.

It is difficult to assess what the trends or major "ah-ha's" are from this list. However, if you use a process where you separate out each individual thought and put them into "like buckets", you will begin to see that the answers make sense. Natural groups appear by themselves.
If you think of the tools you used in kindergarten, you'll get a better idea: You could cut out each thought, represented by a word or sentence into individual slips of paper. Then put all these slips out on a clean table. Then start sorting them into buckets where they belong. If they belong in two buckets, then simply make another copy and put it in both

buckets. Pretty soon, an obvious title for the group will reveal itself to you. Once you have a series of groups with titles, count the number of mentions within each group.

This is an Affinity Diagramming process that can be researched on the web. You've probably used it in your brainstorming sessions. It's just re-purposed for solving an interesting challenge to go from qualitative to quantitative information.

The results of using this process on the list, above is:

Technology   13
Ever-increasingly complex technology
Unsure of which competing technology to use
Backup/Infrastructure
Web Development
Database Structure
Security
Development Architecture
Keeping current with new releases before vendors drop support
Choosing to adapt new technologies that truly have business benefit.
Security and virus protection
Security
Wireless technologies
Merging instances of JDE.

Business-orientation of IT projects   10
Choosing to adapt new technologies that truly have business benefit.
Acquisitions
Demand versus willingness to pay
Managing Executive Management team to provide resources and funding to meet the needs of the business
Decrease in work available
Costs
Licensing costs
Business Intelligence

Meeting the needs of the 404 audit in 2005
Corporate wide standardization of change management and SDLC.

Customer-focus   3
Gaining end user commitment and ownership of projects
Maintaining high levels of support for our customers.
End User reporting.

Managing our human resources   3
Available skills
Too few people for everything that needs to get done
Finding top quality consultants

Project management   3
Project management
Establishment of Project Management Office
Administration

Large-scale projects   3
Integration
Supporting multiple systems
Implementing enterprise apps

Sarbanes Oxley compliance.   3
Sarbanes Oxley compliance.
Sarbanes Oxley compliance.
Compliance with Sarbanes Oxley Act of 2002

Outside "forces"   2
Collaboration with third-parties
Increased competition

The secondary process we are using is to first *analyze* (get into details), and then *synthesize* (integrate the "ah-ha's"). We are looking for insights, not necessarily the most detail.

From this process, you can summarize the groups as such:

Current Challenges	# of mentions	Rating	Cumulative
Technology	13	33%	33%
Business-orientation of IT projects	10	25%	58%
Customer-focus	3	8%	65%
Managing our human resources	3	8%	73%
Project management	3	8%	80%
Large-scale projects	3	8%	88%
Sarbanes Oxley compliance.	3	8%	95%
Outside "forces"	2	5%	100%

As you can see, *just two* of the eight groups account for nearly 60% of the current challenges CIOs are facing. With all the excitement of Sarbanes-Oxley (SOx) compliance, it pales in comparison to the issues of technology (shifting and changing all the time), and Business-orientation of IT projects (as required by the CIO's boss).

Where would *you* start focusing your efforts and messages?

Without this information, my client could have believed all the market noise about SOx compliance and made a terrible decision. Instead, he focused on the facts – *as perceived by customers and prospective customers.*

It is the customers' language that matters. That will sell. That will shorten your sales cycle! In good times and bad.

Cross-correlating answers: Analysis process

Often, it is important to answer the question "How many people aged X through Y live in this or that zip code. The results might look something like:

	Total*	What is your age-range?								
What is your zip code?		Teens	20s	30s	40s	50s	60s	70s	80s	90s+
97006	30.8%	0.0%	0.0%	50.0%	33.3%	0.0%	0.0%	0.0%	0.0%	0.0%
97007	23.1%	0.0%	0.0%	25.0%	16.7%	0.0%	100.0%	0.0%	0.0%	0.0%
97008	23.1%	0.0%	50.0%	25.0%	16.7%	0.0%	0.0%	0.0%	0.0%	0.0%
97124	0.0%	0.0%	0.0%	0.0%	0.0%	0.0%	0.0%	0.0%	0.0%	0.0%
97219	15.4%	0.0%	0.0%	0.0%	33.3%	0.0%	0.0%	0.0%	0.0%	0.0%
97223	7.7%	0.0%	50.0%	0.0%	0.0%	0.0%	0.0%	0.0%	0.0%	0.0%
97229	0.0%	0.0%	0.0%	0.0%	0.0%	0.0%	0.0%	0.0%	0.0%	0.0%

*Total = The number of respondents for the entire survey who answered the Row question and, if a filter is applied, meet the filter criteria.

As you may no doubt understand, the questions you will ask have everything to do with finding out *what you need to know* – in order to reach the right customers (market), speaking their language (message), in the manner that your customers buy (method). To do anything else is guessing, assuming, and just plain crazy. Yet businesses do it all the time.

Conclusions, Recommendations, and Rationale

So, what do you do with all this new information?

Well, what do you want? Significantly more "A" customers! This is the result we want to achieve. We gain this result by the decisions we make and actions we take – to implement what we learned.

Through the analysis process, you will learn the best market, best message(s), and best methods to reach your soon-to-be-many customers. You are doing this to not only attract more of the right customers, but to bring in more revenue *while* reducing your costs *and* sales cycle.

The decisions you make will be based on the knowledge you gain, through the assessment of the information – obtained through the analyses of the data.

This seemingly convoluted thinking is really quite simple, and can be followed via the graphic on the next page:

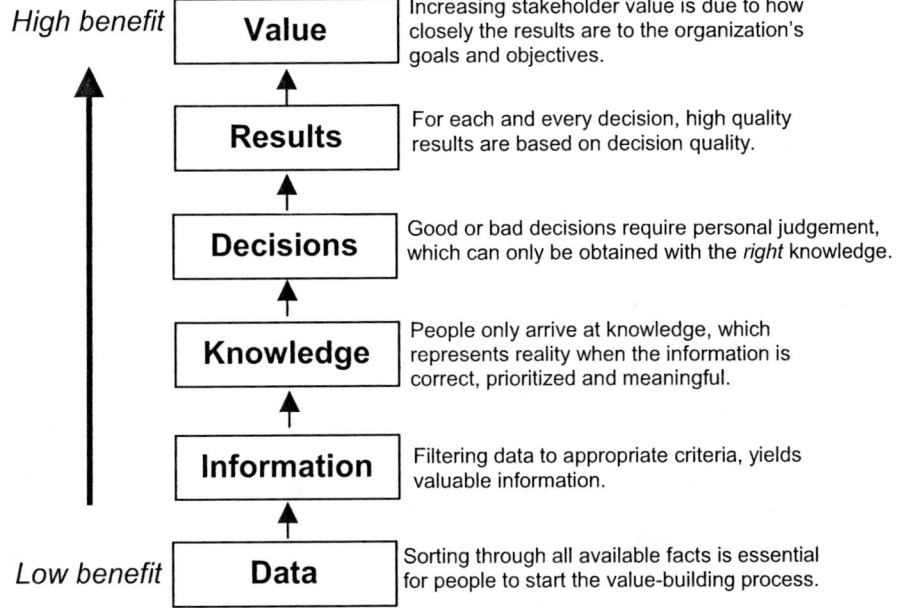

You start with knowing what *you* need to know, then find out (the data). Then work your way up the value chain – through the process outlined in this book.

Let's look at one of the insights we gained by using this process with a client.

> I performed both the internal and external assessments to help a client attract significantly more customers. In their case, they sold through Value-Added Resellers (VARs), so it was important to learn the VAR's language and buying process. In the following table, you will see the results of the "method" portion of the assessment. There are 18 methods, categorized into eight groups, along with the number of times each was mentioned. As you will see, one group (read: method) accounted for nearly 50% of the response, almost three times greater than the next-nearest group.

The top 37.5% of the methods (3 out of 8) account for over 72% of the responses. Advertising garnered exactly 0% and together with PR and direct contact, the bottom 37.5% of methods generated a response of only 12%. You guessed it: the top three methods were six times more effective than the bottom three. It is quite clear what this company should do.

Information sources		#	Rating	Cum
Referrals		28	47%	47%
Referrals from business associates	9			
Clients	8			
Referrals from end-users	7			
Trade Associations	2			
User Groups	2			
Prior experiences		10	17%	63%
Case studies	5			
Testimonials	5			
Web searches		5	8%	72%
Vendor Web site	3			
Web Search	2			
Newsletters		5	8%	80%
Industry Newsletters	5			
Seminars		5	8%	88%
Industry Seminars	5			
PR		4	7%	95%
Magazine articles	4			
Direct Vendor Contacts		3	5%	100%
Calls from vendor sales representative	2			
Vendor Brochures	1			
Direct Mail	0			
Vendor Newsletter	0			
Advertising & trade shows		0	0%	100%
Trade Magazine Advertising	0			
Trade Shows	0			
Total:	60			

Note: There were 10 respondents, which yielded 60 responses.

The story doesn't end there. Because we had also performed the *internal* assessment, we knew exactly how much my client spent on marketing, and could put them into the appropriate groups. We could then calculate how much money they were wasting, and how much more effective their new marketing tactics could be:

Information sources	Rating	Marketing $s	
1 Referrals	47%	$ -	} = 0%
2 Prior experiences	17%	$ -	
3 Web searches	8%	$ 24,250	} = 15%
4 Newsletters	8%	$ -	
5 Seminars	8%	$ -	
6 PR	7%	$ 77,400	
7 Direct Vendor Contacts	5%	$ 6,000	$136,150 = 85%
8 Advertising & trade shows	0%		
Trade Magazine Advertising		$ 9,250	
Trade Shows		$ 43,500	
Total:		$160,400	

Eighty-five percent of their marketing & sales budget went into 12% return, while the other 15% of their marketing & sales budget went into 8% return efforts, and exactly 0% went into the top two tactics, which yielded a 64% (47% + 17%) response rate! When you work out the math, they could be 34 times more effective by simply shifting where they spent their money.

This company was grossing $1 million a year, so they were spending 16% of gross revenue on marketing & sales. Looking at this more closely, we see that they could pocket $136,150 and not have much of an effect on revenue. Or, they could pocket half of this (as net profit improvement) and spend about $70K on the top one or two methods (referral award program, or something that leveraged referrals) and generate at least *double their revenue* in short order. (Note how internal ah-ha's support external insights.)

> This is where all seven secrets come into play. Usually, my client "gets" the information, makes decisions based on what s/he's learned, and reaps the rewards (Addendum #1). In this case, my client did not accept the insights that were derived. He was not open to changing (his mind) about what he should do. He assumed that because his VARs' sales people wanted press clippings, that he should get those (even though his customers [decision-makers] were the VAR CEOs, and we know what they wanted). He didn't recognize the difference between strategic and tactical marketing.
>
> He did not gain the benefit he could have.

Rocket Science

There is an article in the May 23rd, 2005 edition of Forbes Magazine about a former engineer who decided to use statistical analyses to help marketers. I read this with great interest, because I felt he was doing what I was, and was curious.

I discovered that even though he used sophisticated analysis tools (multivariable testing, experimental design, Taguchi methods), the application of these methods did not mimic the strategic nature of the Seven Secrets, nor did they obtain the significant results that could have for a couple reasons. First, the marketing department seemed to be in control – in applying his methods. Their request was on the order of *"How can we make our direct marketing (DM) more effective?"* In that light (with that limitation in thinking only about *one* tactic), the results were impressive, indeed. For that one tactic. He was able to learn how to improve DM response rates from 0.9% to 5.4%, which is near the normal limit for DM. Looking at the prior table (for my client's example),

DM was already about 5%. By taking a *strategic* approach – by asking "How can we improve our (entire) marketing effectiveness?", one starts looking at DM *relative* to other tactics... from the perspective of the customer. Simply changing from DM (5%) to Referral approach (47%), the potential upside was nearly *ten times* that of DM, in the first place, and over 50x if their initial DM was at 0.9%! *This other method costs about $150,000!*

The approach in this book will help you spot multiples *of revenue potential*, not just percentages.

Brainscans and Functional MRIs

There was a 2006 Business Week article (which was carried by many news stations at the time), explaining how some advertising firms were looking at improving advertising response rates. I believe there are some ethical issues about their techniques (subjecting paid participants to have their brains scanned, while looking at different ads).

The notion here is the same as that of the prior example: *"How can we make our ads better?"* Again, this assumes that advertising is the best medium. It may be, but focusing on one tactic and trying to be efficient with that one tactic is not nearly as powerful, nor as valuable to you – as being effective, by learning what the best methods are in the first place. *This method costs between $50,000 and $100,000.*

If anyone is measuring ROI, (for a mid-sized company) the improvements barely justify the expense. And small companies can't afford it. If your are at a large company, the potential improvements by taking a *strategic* view (recommended in this book) could mean hundreds of millions in additional revenue and even profitability.

Focus groups can be too unstructured and rarely "focus" on the things that really matter. Tactical things are typically discussed. And they can cost $5,000 to $50,000 or more (each), depending on the number of groups held.

How would you prefer to spend your money?

One final note on these Secrets: When times are good, companies tend to get complacent. Meaning they don't figure out what they *need* to know: *"Customers are buying, so we must be doing something right!"*

When times turn bad, cash becomes tight, and doing this process seems like it will take too long and cost too much.

However, it is *precisely* during these times when this process is most powerful: By finding out the answers to the questions posed in this book, you will *know* so much more about your prospective customers, that you will be able to outperform your competitors and grow – even in bad economic times!

Secret #7
Test Your Assumptions

Even though one of the secrets is to assume nothing, we all do. No one can know everything. We learned so much from the internal and external assessments, that we need to test what we've learned, so we can further reduce our assumptions.

One of the main benefits of following the process outlined in this book is that you will be able to define your assumptions and then reduce them (Secret #3). Just by recognizing you are making assumptions (because you're being open to learning a new language - Secret #2), right away your level of assumptions will drop.

Plotting your assumptions over time may look something like this:

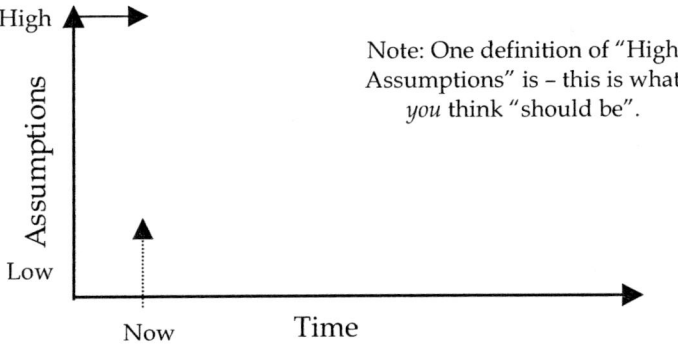

Note: One definition of "High Assumptions" is – this is what *you* think "should be".

"High" means *relative* to where I want you to end up, not necessarily relative to other people.

Without being open to change, assumptions will likely remain:

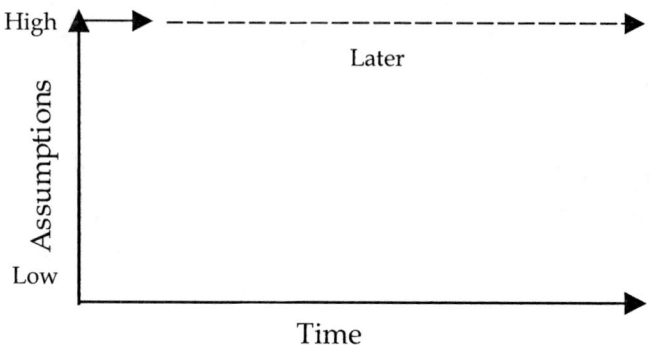

After performing an internal assessment (Secret #5), you will gain insights, which means you're learning valuable information upon which to base decisions. In this case, your assumptions get replaced with knowledge, so they go down over time:

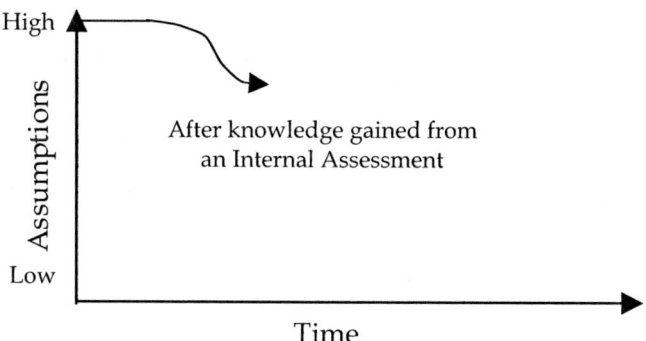

You can gain significantly more valuable information about your customers by performing an External Assessment (Secret #6). Once completed, you will again reduce your assumptions:

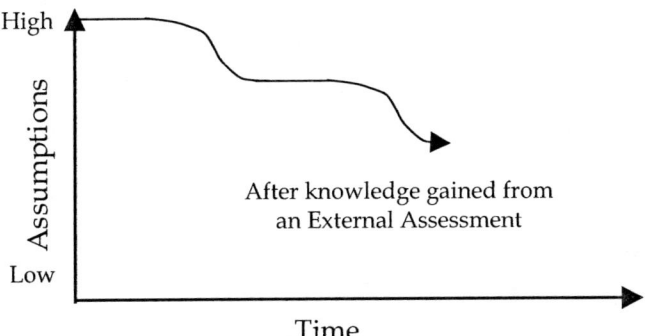

The next step is to test out your assumptions. If you realize that you may still be making assumptions (because there's no proof yet that what you've learned will actually attract significantly more customers), then it is essential to test your decisions. Before spending a bundle. Your assumptions will decrease further:

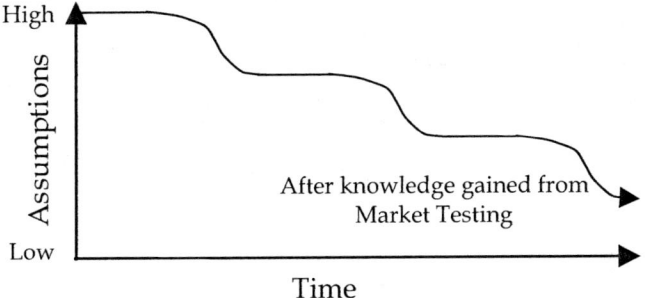

The amazing thing is… people (understand and) pay money for what "is", versus what "should be".

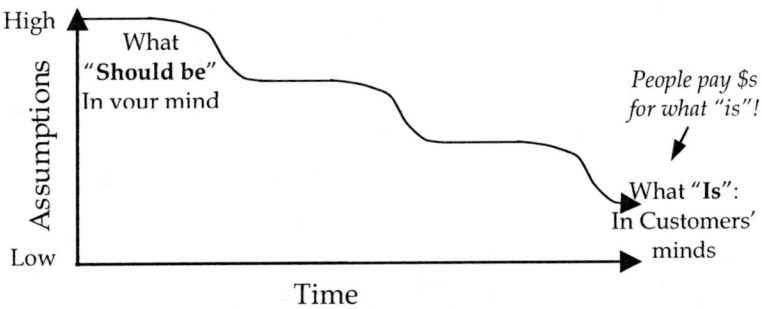

Once you learn your customers' language (Secrets #4 & #6), by testing what you've learned through a methodical approach, you will be able to discuss with them - what "is". And then measure the return on investment of your new marketing tactics.

Once you compare current performance against your prior performance (learned from the Internal Assessment), you will be *able* to know how much better your new approach "is". If it is worse, you can stop before spending too much time and money. However, it will likely be significantly better.

To summarize, there are three things you can fine tune if the new ROI is worse than the old ROI:

1. _____
2. _____
3. _____

Yes, this is a quiz. What are the three things?

The three areas that you have control over is:

1. The *market* you focus on – your "A" customers.
2. Your *message* – that resonates with these customers.
3. The *method* you employ to reach them – how they buy.

Once you know these three things, you will be able to attract significantly more "A" customers – much more cost-effectively.

How many more? That depends on your industry, market, product & service quality, etc. And it will depend on how well you implement what you learn.

To find out how some companies have benefited by implementing this entire process, go to Addendum 1: Real-World Examples.

How to Attract Significantly More Customers... in good times & bad

Bonus Secret
Implement & Follow-through!

But wait! There's more!

The concepts in this book mean nothing if they are not implemented, with the appropriate follow-though.

> One of Synergy Consulting Group's clients, who implemented these concepts, briefly benefited as a result. They doubled the number of customers and their average $100,000 per month gross revenue increased to over $170,000 in less than six months (three months after completing the process). They were focused on the recommendations of Synergy's report, which determined – through the steps in this book – exactly what they needed to focus on: Market, Message, and Method.
>
> After eight or nine months, the company's revenue dropped off. When I checked in with them, the CEO & I discussed the top recommendations in the report, and how they were doing with them.
>
> The company "forgot" and started focusing on operational issues at the expense of the lessons learned – and therefore the required organizational behavior – to continue the significant upward growth in customer-attraction.
>
> Only by re-focusing their effort, did they start increasing revenue again.
>
> Another client went through this process in 2004. What they learned did not align with "who they were". Specifically, they were not "sales" types. They avoided the findings of what the process told them, which was [1] Provide samples, [2] To businesses, [3] Explain the business reasons for giving their

(extremely high-quality, excellent-tasting) products to clients, employees, vendors, and strategic partners.

It was only after they faced going out of business (in 2007) that they implemented the recommendations. Perhaps to little too late, but they did have success – and sent me this card:

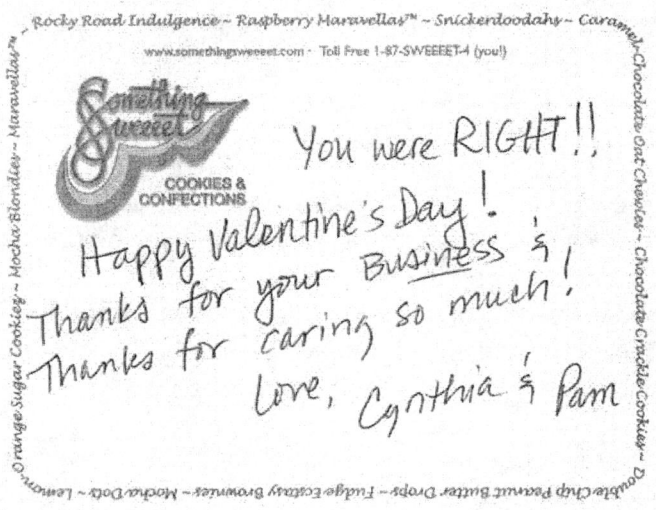

The fact is: *I* wasn't right... the *results of the research* were right. I just happened to know how to figure it out. Now you do, too!

A second "bonus secret" is this: Whatever you do, do **not** get taken in by BOGGSAT! It is one of the worst things you can do! BOGGSAT = Bunch of Guys & Gals Sitting Around Talking. Getting together your management / executive team members to brainstorm / figure out "what to do next" results in a bunch of (potentially great) ideas, but it cannot substitute for doing the hard work of *getting in the mind* of your customers. These ideas usually include: "Let's try this. Or that." These are tactics, not strategies. They will yield the same unpredictable results.

There is a direct correlation between focusing your efforts in the highest-ROI direction (or not), and the resultant return on investment you achieve. Retreating to old habits (BOGGSAT & tactics) will get you old results.

Addendum 1
Real-world Examples

The examples in this book have been sanitized, but they are real none-the-less. There is absolutely no guarantee that your company will achieve these results because your company and market are different and you are different. However, these results are an indication of what you can strive for.

Remember, if you identify areas where you could increase your ROI 20x to 30x, and have some difficulties in implementation, you may still achieve 2x or 3x in a matter of 3 to 24 months!

For the examples provided below, each of the Internal and External Assessment reports were 20 to 40 pages long, with 10 to 20 (or more) recommendations. In no way are these examples able to convey the depth and details of the engagements, nor the insights found. They are provided to communicate a general "quality" and high-level summary of the improvements made as a result of implementing the Seven Secrets.

The length of time it takes to implement these secrets vary. It may take a long time to come to grips with the "personal" secrets, in which case you won't be ready for the "business" secrets to even begin. However, once you are able to start the Internal and External Assessments, it may take between 2 to 3 months before knowing exactly what you need to know to make the absolute best decisions anyone could make. It may take another 3 to 6 months before seeing significant improvements. And in some cases, it may take up to 2 years. It depends on you *and* your marketplace.

To the real-world examples:

Client #1

Situation

Size of company:	$2.8 million/year; $233K/month.
# of employees:	22.
Issue / situation:	Product company. Great international sales, limited success in the U.S. Competitors had surpassed the company. Found out 3 months into the assignment that client wanted to sell the company. Had 4 prior acquisition offers, the best of which was $1 million.

Application of Seven Secrets

CEO:	Ready to do what was needed.
Internal assessment:	Discovered their primary marketing ROI performance: $1 (marketing expense) bought 50 cents – for U.S. customers.
External assessment:	Determined true "language" of customers, as well as their motivation and preferred method of buying.
Effort:	Implemented recommendations from facts uncovered through internal / external assessments.

Results

Additional revenue:	$500K more in 3 months.
ROI of new message / method:	$1 (marketing expense) bought $40 of revenue: Increase of 80x.
Price of product:	Increased from $15K to $80K (Immediately after learning about the value to client's customer.)

Value of company:	Acquired for $17 million (including cash, equity swap and with earn-out provisions).
Time frame:	Six months.
# of external survey responses required:	17.

Client #2

Situation

Size of company:	$1.2 million/year; $100K/month
# of employees:	16.
Issue / situation:	Service company, which was "porpoising": Revenue was going up then down then up, then down. No real repeatable marketing / sales process.

Application of Seven Secrets

CEO:	Appeared ready to do what was needed.
Internal assessment:	No sales funnel. No repeatable marketing efforts: CEO would make sales calls.
External assessment:	Referrals were the primary way customers bought: Each customer had up to 100 more "reviewers" in the company that could be cost-effectively reached, with the right message that was determined.
Effort:	Initially implemented recommendations from facts uncovered through internal / external assessments.

Results

Additional customers:	2X.
Additional revenue:	$71K more per month: 71% increase.
Time frame:	Six months.
Additional info:	After 6 months, revenue dipped. Upon further discussion, client reverted back to old ways, putting out "fires" instead of continuing to implement what was needed. Upon recognizing this, company revenue increased again.
# of external survey responses required:	9.

Client #3

Situation

Size of company:	$2.9 million/year; $242K/month.
# of employees:	43.
Issue / situation:	Product company. Great product & team. No real processes nor organizational maturity. ROI of marketing efforts unknown. Cost to acquire customers, unknown. One product being sold, working on 38 products – none of which were making progress.

Application of Seven Secrets

CEO:	Open to trying something new.
Internal assessment:	Other than focus groups (did not provide reliable information), no market-assessment processes.
External assessment:	Determined message that resonated and preferred method of buying.

Effort: Implemented recommendations from facts uncovered through internal / external assessments.

Results
Revenue:	> $5 million.
# of employees:	58.
New products:	Eight more products & services that met identified customers' needs.
Price of product:	Increased from $795 to $1395K
Value of company:	Increased from 13 cents / share to 58 cents/share. Company raised $23 million from investors.
Time frame:	Eighteen months.
# of external survey responses required:	25.

Client #4

Situation
Size of company:	Start-up.
# of employees:	2.
Issue / situation:	Product company. Excellent products. Just starting out, fewer than 200 customers.

Application of Seven Secrets
CEOs:	Open to trying something new.
Internal assessment:	Determined their *business* customers were worth over 4x their *consumer* customers.

External assessment:	Determined customers bought due to referral and that sampling products increased their likelihood to buy several-fold.
Effort:	Initially implemented recommendations from facts uncovered through internal / external assessments.

Results

Revenue:	Year over year increases 80% first 6 months.
# of customers:	Increased 112% in six month, now at nearly 800 customers – a 400% increase.
Time frame:	Six months for initial increase.
# of external survey responses required:	16.

Addendum 2
Seven Secrets Summarized

1. **Recognize the Difference Between Strategic and Tactical Marketing**
   Ensure that you know the difference between "doing stuff" and "getting results".

2. **Be 100% Open to Change & Learning**
   Otherwise, you will get what you've always got.

3. **Assume Nothing**
   None of us is as smart as all of us.

4. **Recognize You May Need to Learn a New Language**
   Your customers'.

5. **Assess Your Company's Current Performance**
   Manage (make decisions) by fact.

6. **Ask Your Customers / Prospects What *You* Need to Know**
   Only *then* can you know what will sell.

7. **Test Your Assumptions**
   Find out what "is".

Addendum 3
How to Get Your Data Analyzed

If you are able to collect data outlined in either Secrets # 5 or #6, and would prefer to have them analyzed by Synergy Consulting Group, we can do that.

You will need to save your data in Excel format ('97). For each analysis, you will need to go to www.synergy-usa.com/analysisoptions.htm and click on "Get the ball rolling" and send your spreadsheet, via the email address located at www.synergy-usa.com/contact.htm.

We will review it to see if it can be analyzed and if not, what you will need to do to make it "workable" and send that to you via your valid email address.

Once we agree that it is workable, you will need to go www.synergy-usa.com/analysisoptions.htm and select an option that meets your needs. (We will need to talk before doing so.) You will receive an analyzed spreadsheet back via email within the time-frame stated on the website; most likely a couple of days – depending on the complexity of your spreadsheet and our workload.

How to Attract Significantly More Customers... in good times & bad

Addendum 4
Products & Services to Help You Grow Your Company

The Entrepreneur's Survival Guide (Book)

If you are looking to overcome difficult business challenges, this book can save you significant time & money. Whether you are an entrepreneur, small business owner or CEO of a medium-sized company trying to take your company to its next several levels. *Order the new edition today!*

Seven Secrets: How to Attract Significantly More Customers! (Audio CD)

This audio CD provides a refresher of the book, including new insights and questions / answers in the live presentation.

How to survive and thrive in challenging times (Audio CD)

Learn the Top 10 ways companies fail and the Top 10 ways companies never get off the ground! And what you can do to overcome challenges you may have.

How to Help Investors Buy Into Your High-Growth Company. (Spreadsheet)

If investors are telling you "no", perhaps you need to learn their language. Often, entrepreneurs have difficulty communicating how investors will gain from their investment. One way to overcome this resistance is to develop your "capitalization table" in way that resonates with investors. If you want help getting to 'Yes!', you may want to get to a working cap table, first.

How to speed time-to-market (Monogram)

Are you looking to dramatically decrease your time-to-market? Are you interested in accurately predicting your project's probable schedule? Buy the "Earned Value" Monogram. 30-page White Paper.

Go to www.synergy-usa.com/newproducts.htm, today!

Acknowledgements

The author would like to thank the following people:

First and foremost is my family:
Sylvia, Nicole, Nathan and Michael, and our extended family.

Other who have helped in so many ways:
My mentors: Dean Baker, Joe Berg, Steve Bonkowski, Shel Bresin, Virginia Mort, Richard Odum, Margo Parker & Mike Peron. Also, Ed Benthale, Robert Campbell, William Campbell, Michael Coates, Ed Clark, Debi Coleman, Don Eakin, Dick Ekstrom, Wayne Embree, Les Fahey, Jim Franceus, Steve Freiling, Mrs. Fulton, Tom Godfrey, Larry Hughes, Steve Jaynes, Gene Kinsel, Richard Lindberg, Ross & Rosalie Macdonald, Carol Mason, Frank McNabb, Blane Meier, Brad Paul, Eric Pozzo, Pat Quinn, Frank Reyes, John Sechrest, Michael Shenker, Tom Sneed, Joe Stopper, Zim Troutt, Chuck Wagner, Greg & Tracey Warnke, Jim Wes, Linda Weston, & Patrick Wheeler. Those at OTBC with whom I've worked: Pete Decher, David Eastman, Elia Freedman, Rob Gardier, Frank Hall, Dwayne Johnson, Wm Leler, Bart Massey, Mark Owen, Karen Petersen, LaVonne Reimer, Iris Sasaki, & Colleen Becker, and many more! Thanks to Steve Morris & Dennis Powers, especially! Bob Bredemeier (www.bobbredemeier.com) created the cover, and his students are great!

Those who purchased my first book in quantity – for others:
Dr. Thorsten Egelkraut (OSU's Agri-Business/Management), Summit Financial Advisors, Nancy Isely-Fletcher (MIT Enterprise Forum's Venture Labs), Dr. Aaron Johnson (OSU's Food Innovation Center), Blane Meier (Summit Financial Advisors), Dr. Robert Wiltbank (Willamette University).

Organizations who have invited me to speak / printed excerpts:
Beaverton Chamber of Commerce, Cedar Mill Business Association, CEO Refresher, Corvallis BizNet Group, Decisioneering (Oracle), Hillsboro Chamber of Commerce, Indiana Information Technology Association, Lake Oswego Business Alliance, Lake Oswego Chamber of Commerce, North East Ohio Software Association, Oregon Entrepreneur's Network, OregonStartups.com, OTBC, Pacific Continental Bank, Portland State Business Accelerator, Small Business Development Center, Software Association of Oregon , Software Council of Southern California, Software Development Forum, The Alternative Board, VisionSite, Washington Mutual, & Xenium Resources.

And of course, my clients:
www.synergy-usa.com/clients.htm

About the Author

Mark Paul has thirty years of business and leadership experience in bootstrapped start-ups through Global 500 corporations, in consulting, executive and interim executive roles. He is Managing Partner at **Synergy Consulting Group, LLC** (www.synergy-usa.com). He has held several interim executive roles, including Chief Operating Officer at a software company; President of an "Internet company", and CEO of a public telecom company. He's dramatically increased shareholder value for many companies, located funding and helped more than a few people become millionaires: by building their companies, creating jobs and producing wealth for stockholders.

Prior to consulting, Mark spent eleven years at Ford and Northrop Corporations. He was a senior executive at Northrop Corporation; building a multi-million dollar business unit in two years, where he led between four & 250 people in "line" and project roles. He was awarded U.S. Patent # 4,631,583, for a software-controlled electro-optical device, has a degree in Physics from the University of California, Irvine, post-graduate studies in technology management at Cal-Tech, and has board-level experience. He wrote several editions of *"The Entrepreneur's Survival Guide"* and has published numerous articles – to help domestic and international businesses.

In his spare time, he plays guitar and has produced several CDs (www.aphasia-music.com). He is particularly interested in renewable energy (www.energy2025.com) and international business. His wife of 30 years and three children are his reasons for living. He can be reached by visiting his website at www.synergy-usa.com.

What Do Others Say?

"I believe any CEO - whether from a startup or a large corporation - can gather valuable strategic insights from this book. Insights that translate into action, which directly improves both the top line and bottom-line. I've seen Mark Paul apply these principles to several resident ventures at the incubator for high-tech startups. If you want to attract significantly more customers, this book will help you get there."
        Steve Morris – Executive Director of
        Oregon's Technology Business Incubator

"Mark brings significant value to CEOs and business owners: In just one meeting he developed an innovative and concrete way, providing upwards of $500,000 of value."
        Tyson Planz – Owner of Capital Connection

"I now understand my customer's needs, the sales cycle and the target market better. Mark added significant value to the strategic direction of my company."
        Steve Werner – President of Rapid Transform

"I can't help but wonder how much further along we would be today if we would have started working with you a year ago!"
        Elia Freedman – CEO of Infinity Softworks

"I would wholeheartedly recommend Mark to anyone who wants to stop wasting time and make their marketing dollars work! I don't know why any business owner wouldn't use his services!"
        Dave Griffiths – Owner of Freedom, Inc.

"Mark visibly and dramatically improved the condition of the organization. I've seen him lead high-level strategy sessions and then roll-up his sleeves to lead the successful implementation of those strategies. Consider Mark Paul your point-man when it's time to clarify, navigate and implement your short, and long-term objectives."
        Mark Effinger – CEO of RichContent.com

"Mark is the guy you need if you want to quickly get to the core reasons why your business is not firing on all cylinders. I hired him and he hit it right on all counts."
    Doug Van Riper – CEO of Sales Resource Group

"Mark has an exceptionally keen eye in helping clients find value in a broad spectrum of business. I'd recommend Mark to any company."
    John Skardon – CEO of Salmon Creek Consulting

"Thank you for presenting your seminar 'Seven Secrets: How to Attract More Customers'. You did not talk about the "same-old" marketing and sales tactics, rather, how to cost-effectively attract the best customers, yielding the highest return on investment."
    Carol Mason – Director, Portland State Business Accelerator

"Mark is a class act. He is very client driven - having the skills and knowledge to identify, formulate and implement marketing strategies."
    Peter Paskill – Business owner CareerMakers,
        acquired by HR Answers, Inc.

"Mark is a strategic thinker, adept at creating opportunities to improve or turn-around businesses."
    Janet Johnson – Marketing executive

"I highly recommend Mark Paul without hesitation!"
    Mark Boyd – Co-Founder/Board Member, Chrome Systems Inc.

"Your advice is especially valuable."
    Fred Phillips – Managing Partner of General Informatics

"It is for those CEOs who really want to get to the next level - and it requires openness to challenge the status quo. …helped us achieve growth at a 40%+ rate and increasing profitability by 75%."
    John Boone – CEO of EmploymentTrends,
        acquired by SOS Staffing, Inc.

"We quadrupled our student body within the first couple of years after your consulting services!"
    Wes Jarrell – Department Chair: Oregon Graduate Institute, ESE